English for the
World of Work

by
Carolyn W. Knox

AGS®

American Guidance Service, Inc.
Circle Pines, Minnesota 55014-1796
800-328-2560

About the Author

Carolyn W. Knox received her undergraduate degree from Towson State University and her master's degree from Loyola College. She has also done considerable course work at American University, Temple University, and Johns Hopkins University. Mrs. Knox has served 27 years in the Baltimore City Public Schools as a secondary English teacher, demonstration teacher, and English department head. She was also a supervisor of English and elementary language arts, head of English textbook adoption, and director of English and language arts curriculum production. In addition to learning packages, workbooks, and textbooks, Mrs. Knox has written critiques and other materials as a consultant for several leading educational publishing houses.

Photo Credits: All photographs by James L. Shaffer

Printed in the United States of America

ISBN 0-7854-0859-2-H (hardcover)

ISBN 0-7854-0860-6-S (softcover)

Product Number 90090 (hardcover)

Product Number 90091 (softcover)

A 0 9 8 7 6 5 4 3 2 1

Contents

Chapter

1

Finding Your Career

Throughout your life you probably will have to look for several jobs. Before you graduate, you may have to look for part-time jobs after school, and after you graduate, you will have to look for a full-time job. There are some skills that you can learn that will make finding these jobs a little easier.

In Chapter 1, you will find important information that will help you find a job.

Goals for Learning

▶ To learn how to read help-wanted ads in the newspaper

▶ To be able to determine if you qualify for a particular job

▶ To be able to decide if a particular job is suitable for you

▶ To understand the different services offered at employment agencies and job placement offices

1

Classified ads

Advertisements that are listed in the newspaper in different groups; for example, ads for cars would be listed together, ads for pets in another section, and job openings in another.

Maria Rodriguez needed a full-time job. The jobs she had had before were part-time jobs that she had found by reading signs in store windows. Now she wanted to use the computer skills she had learned in high school to find a permanent job. Her friends told her to read the **classified ads** in the newspaper and to go to job placement centers. When Maria looked at the **help-wanted ads** in the newspaper, she wished she understood them better.

Help-wanted ads sometimes can be confusing if they include unfamiliar terms and **abbreviations**. In her local newspaper, Maria saw this help-wanted ad. Are there any words in this ad that you do not understand?

Help-wanted ads

Advertisements for employment or job openings.

ne	**DATA ENTRY CLERK** Fast	g
e	growing pipe, valve & fitting	$
e	distributor loc on W side. Ability	fo
lp	to use wd. proc. prog. a must.	lo
—	Call Ms. Goodman, Mon. or	re
·s	Tues. 8-10 a.m., 555-4857.	he
ne		

Abbreviations

The shortened forms of written words; for example, req. for required.

Although Maria understood that the ad was for a data entry clerk for a distributor of pipes, valves, and fittings, she wasn't sure what the abbreviations *loc* and *W side* meant. She decided to ask her friend Tony for some help.

"Tony, would you read this ad for a data entry clerk to me?" she asked. "It may be a job I can do, but I'm not sure."

"Sure, Maria," answered Tony. "The ad says that a business located on the west side of town wants to hire a data entry clerk. You must be able to use word processing programs."

"Do you think that the company would count part-time experience?" asked Maria.

"I don't know. Why don't you call Ms. Goodman and ask her? You can call Monday or Tuesday between 8 o'clock and 10 o'clock in the morning."

Tony was able to make sense out of the ad because he understood the terms and abbreviations in it. You will also need to be able to do the same thing when you are looking for a job.

Activity A Number your paper 1 to 3. Then read these three ads and write the meaning of each underlined word.

1)
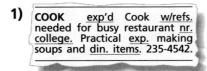

COOK   exp'd Cook w/refs. needed for busy restaurant nr. college. Practical exp. making soups and din. items. 235-4542.

2)

SALES

Nat'l co, high comm. New product. No exp. nec.
Mon.
555-8695.

3)

MAINTENANCE ASS'T.   Must have a least 3 yrs. exp. in htg. and AC. All phases of maintenance nec.   542-4891.

Activity B Number your paper 1 to 13. Then match each abbreviated phrase in the first column with its meaning in the second column.

Words	Meanings
1) exp'd.	**a)** high commission
2) w/refs.	**b)** with references
3) nr. college	**c)** no experience necessary
4) exp.	**d)** call 555-8695 on Monday
5) din. items	**e)** assistant
6) ASS'T.	**f)** experienced
7) 3 yrs. exp.	**g)** three years experience
8) htg. and AC	**h)** national company
9) nec.	**i)** heating and air conditioning
10) Nat'l co	**j)** near college
11) high comm.	**k)** dinner items
12) No exp. nec.	**l)** necessary
13) Mon. 555-8695	**m)** experience

More Abbreviations in Help-Wanted Ads

There are other terms and abbreviations that you and Maria may need to know before you can fully understand some help-wanted ads. Study this list carefully.

aft.	afternoon	lic.	license
agcy.	agency	mfg.	manufacturing
avail.	available	min.	minimum
beg.	beginning	pd.	paid
bene.	benefits	pos.	position
comp.	computer	pref.	preferred
des.	desired	proc.	processing
ed.	education	prog.	program
eve.	evenings	p/t	part time
exc.	excellent	req.	required
f/t	full time	sal.	salary
grad.	graduate	trng.	training
incl.	including/included	20K	$20,000
ins.	insurance	wd.	word

Activity C Number your paper 1 to 3. Then rewrite these ads by changing the abbreviations to full words.

1)

DRIVER Lic. req. Must work aft. & eve. Sal. and tips. Ins. and other bene. provided.
757-0853

2)

P/T CLERK
Mfg. co. Will provide trng. Beg. min. wage. Exp. pref. Hrs. 2-6 aft. 477-3745

3)

SECRETARY Pos. avail for h.s. grad with exp. Sal. 20K incl. pd. vacation and ed. bene. Must wk. f/t and some eve.
569-7588

Along with understanding the terms and abbreviations used in the help-wanted ads, you also need to know how these ads are organized in most newspapers. As you learned in the last section, the help-wanted ads are located in the classified part of the newspaper in the "Help Wanted" or "Employment" section. Within that section the jobs are listed in **alphabetical order**; for example, *artist* would come before *clerk*, and *janitor* would come before *server*.

> **Alphabetical order**
>
> *Arranged in the order of the letters of the alphabet (A, B, C, etc.).*

CLASSIFIED ADVERTISING
Employment

HELP WANTED 905	**HELP WANTED** 905	**MISCELL**
ADMINISTRATIVE SECY This top Co. needs polished sect'l talents! Good skills and figure aptitude. 837-0778.	**CHEF-PASTRY** 4 yrs. exp. required, knowledge of European pastry pref. Send résumé to BOX CS 47822	**COUCH AND** good cond.
AIR COND & HEAT PUMP MECHANIC Fully exp. only. Call Frosty Refrig. Mondays, 747-2024.	**CLERICAL** If you love to type, my firm needs your skills. Excellent salary & benefits. Call Lisa 539-5804	**DOG HOUSE** first home fo
AUTO SALESPERSON Sell and make big money on cars and trucks. Salary plus comm. Benefits. 466-1320	**COMPUTER OPERATOR** Must have know. of Cobol lang. and other comp. lang. and be able to use var. comp. software progs. Call 9-5 at 358-TYPE.	**VIDEO GAM** games. 2 cor gun, cleanin **PAPASAN** co $150/obo. K range, $75. a
BOOKKEEPER Comp. exp. nec. Dependable. 675-1118	**DATA ENTRY CLERK** General data entry, 5 days, vic. Smallwood St. 566-5806	**REFRIGERATC** excellent wor

Look for the help-wanted ads in the classified section of your newspaper. You will find ads for such jobs as dental assistants, mechanics, nurses, secretaries, and computer operators. Also notice how these ads are listed in alphabetical order.

What Is Alphabetical Order?

Because the help-wanted ads are listed in alphabetical order, jobs that start with *A* would be listed first, jobs that start with *B* would be listed next, and so on.

A B C D E F G H I J K L M N O P Q R S T U V W X Y Z

Activity A   Rewrite these words in alphabetical order.

tailor	craftsworker	artisan	librarian
driller	farmer	mechanic	programmer
rater	server	auditor	janitor
evaluator	woodworker	bartender	helper
guard	orderly		

When several jobs start with the same letter, look at the second letter. For example, if *bookkeeper* and *bartender* are two jobs in the ads, *bartender* would be listed first because the second letter is *a*. *Bookkeeper* would come after *bartender* because the second letter is *o*. If the first two letters are the same, you have to look at the third letter, and so on.

If several job titles have more than one word and the first words are the same, look at the second word. For example, if one ad is for *auto mechanic* and another is for an *auto attendant*, *auto attendant* would come first because the second word begins with *a*.

Maria uses alphabetical order to locate jobs in the help-wanted ads and to look up company names in the Yellow Pages.

Activity B   Rewrite these words in alphabetical order.

mechanic	janitor	salesperson	machinist
secretary	carpenter	milliner	plumber
biller	chef	stenographer	buyer

When alphabetizing, remember that if the second letters are the same, look at the third letter, and so on. However, when first words are the same, look at the second word.

Activity C Rewrite these words and phrases in alphabetical order.

sales
engineer, industrial
secretarial lab aide
computer specialist
dry cleaner
secretary
engineer, civil
auto salesperson

computer programmer
auto mechanic
engineer, electrical
secretarial assistant
engineer, mechanical
executive director
administrative assistant
auto repairs

Telephone directory

A book or collection of names, addresses, and telephone numbers.

The Skill of Alphabetizing

Being able to alphabetize is an important skill. It not only will help you locate information in the classified ads, but you will find many other uses for it as well. For example, the names in a **telephone directory** and the businesses described in the **Yellow Pages** are listed in alphabetical order. Store directories, **reference books** like dictionaries and encyclopedias, book catalogs in libraries, rows of seats in an auditorium, compact discs in music stores, and street directories are all listed in alphabetical order.

Yellow Pages

The section of a telephone book that lists businesses in alphabetical order by kind of business; for example, you would find the names and telephone numbers of all places to eat under the heading Restaurants.

Activity D Rewrite these job titles from the help-wanted section of a newspaper in alphabetical order.

ENGINEER, ELECTRICAL
SALESPERSON
GUARD
RECEPTIONIST
CLAIMS SUPERVISOR
RETAIL SALESPERSON
ELECTRICIAN
DIETITIAN
RESEARCH ASSISTANT
DATA ENTRY CLERK
CLERK
ANIMAL HANDLER
ENGINEER, CHEMICAL
ENGINEER, MANUFACTURING

Reference books

Books containing useful facts or information— such as a dictionary, encyclopedia, or atlas.

You are now familiar with the abbreviations used in help-wanted ads, and you know that the ads are arranged in alphabetical order in the newspaper. Now some practice reading and understanding these ads probably would be helpful. Think about Maria Rodriguez again. Although she has had some word processing experience, not every ad for a data entry clerk will be a job that she can do or even one that she would want to do.

Activity A Number your paper 1 to 9. Then after you read these ads, answer the questions below them.

1) CLERK   Gen. off. duties and proofrdg. Must have good grammar and word processing skills. Apply in person 9-4 p.m. 20 E Main St.

3) **CLERK**
No exp. nec. Will train. 40-hr wk. Mon-Fri 8 to 4. Many bene. inc. health ins. Call Mr. Merton 555-1921.

2) CLERK   Comp. ex. req., math aptitude a must. Typ. req. Send letter of application by fax to Jeanna Santiago at 555-1632.

1) Which job requires good word processing skills?

2) Which job should you apply for in person?

3) What is meant by *good grammar skills* in the first ad?

4) Which job should you apply for by fax?

5) Which job requires an ability to proofread?

6) Which job requires good math skills?

7) Which ad describes a benefit the employee will receive?

8) How would you send your letter when applying for the job described in the second ad?

9) How would you apply for the job in the third ad?

Activity B Number your paper 1 to 2. Then rewrite these ads in your own words.

1)

SALES
Outside sales in off. equip. Sal. and comm. Co. bene. Call Sally, **555-4943**

2)

AUTO SALES Immed. pos. Exp. pref. Exc. pay plan & bene. Call for appt. 934-1012.

Lesson **4**   **Do I Qualify for This Job?**

In order to use the help-wanted ads wisely, you shouldn't waste your time applying for jobs that you're not qualified for. For example, Maria Rodriguez has had experience as a sales clerk and a receptionist. She also has word processing skills. However, she is not very good in math, and she never learned to do spreadsheets on a computer. As a result, when she looks at ads, she shouldn't bother with the ones that say the applicant must be good in math or the ones that say the person needs to be able to do spreadsheets on a computer.

How will you know if you are qualified for a particular job? The answers to these questions will help you decide whether or not you should apply.

1. Do I have the education required?

2. Can I work the hours and days listed?

3. Do I have the skills needed?

4. Am I able to work the machinery needed for this job?

5. Can I use the tools needed to do this job?

6. Do I have all the other requirements needed for this job?

Is This Job Suitable for Me?

When you apply for a job, you need to think about the pleasure or satisfaction that working at that job could bring day after day. You should also consider if this is the kind of job that you would like to do. Then ask yourself these questions. Their answers will help you decide whether or not a particular job is suitable for you.

> 1. Is this the kind of job that I will enjoy doing?
> 2. Will I make enough money to meet my needs and to make me feel good about the work I'm doing?
> 3. Can I get to this place easily so that I am never late?

Salary

A fixed amount of money paid on a regular basis for work done.

Benefits

Payments or services provided for the workers by a company; for example, vacations, retirements, and health insurance.

Find the help-wanted ads in your newspaper. After you read some of the ads, use the questions on page 9 to help you decide whether or not you are qualified for the jobs. Then use the questions in this section to decide if any of the jobs are suitable for you. Of course, you may not be able to answer all these questions because employers do not always list **salary**, complete **benefits** such as vacations or insurance, chances for advancement, and other such information.

Maria was glad she found a job that she enjoyed and that offered her a good salary and benefits.

Activity A   After you read this help-wanted ad, read about the three people described below. Then decide which person is best qualified to do the job. Be ready to discuss the reasons for your decision.

he	**ASST. CARPENTER'S HELPER** No exp. nec. Must have knowlege of tools and talent for this kind of work. Perm. pos. Opp. for advancement to good worker. Must have driver's lic. Apply in person. Ace Company, 115 Orange Street.	g($5
e		
p		fo
		lo(
on		re
		he

1) Leroy enjoys working with his hands. He knows how to use most tools and fixes all the small appliances in his home. In addition to having a license to drive a car, he also lives on a bus line that goes right by the Ace Company. It would take him about 30 minutes to get there. He can work any hours.

2) Myra went to a vocational school and majored in carpentry. She is skilled with most of the tools used by a carpenter. She has a car and can drive to the Ace Company in about 35 minutes. If she has to take the bus, it will take her an hour. She can work any hours that the company requests.

3) Carlos needs a job. He can use simple tools. He really likes meeting people and working with them. He has a car and a license and can get to the Ace Company in about 15 minutes. He is not sure that he will like this job, but he needs to earn some money.

Employment agency

A company that is in business to help people find jobs.

Job placement office

A city or state office where a person can get help in finding a job.

Maria Rodriguez thought about going to an **employment agency** or to a **job placement office**. These places are in business to help people find jobs. However, most employment agencies charge a fee that must be paid after you have been hired. That fee can be as much as ten percent of your first year's pay. The fee is usually paid by the person looking for the job although sometimes the employer offers to pay it. Before you sign with an agency, make sure you find out who pays the fee and what the fee is. You may find that it is worth paying a fee to get a job. However, if you cannot afford a fee, stay away from an agency where the fee is paid by the employee.

The best way to find an employment agency is to look in the Yellow Pages of your telephone directory. Many agencies specialize in only certain kinds of jobs, and many of the ads will also state whether the employee or the employer pays the fee.

Activity A   Number your paper 1 to 5. Then after you read this ad, answer the following questions.

JOB SEARCH, INC.

For assistance in your office and for professional job placement

• **Stenographers**   *"Fee paid*
• **Bookkeepers**   *by employers"*
• **Receptionists**
• **Data entry / Word Processing**

2313 Kansas Street   **555-1438**

1) Could this agency help you find a job as an automobile mechanic?

2) Maria Rodriguez knows word processing. Would this agency be able to help her find a job?

3) Would Maria have to pay the agency's fee?

4) What is the name of this agency? Where is it located?

5) What telephone number should Maria call to get more information?

Job Placement Offices

Most states and many large cities have job placement offices that can help you find a job without paying a fee. At these offices you can fill out an application and talk with a **counselor**. The counselor will give you advice and work with you to help you find a job.

The United States government also has an Office of Personnel Management where you can apply for jobs within the government. However, most government jobs require that you take a test. The telephone numbers of these kinds of job placement offices are listed in the blue section of your telephone directory.

Maria went to her state's job placement office. She found that she could get all kinds of help there at no charge at all. Here are some of the services that most city and state job placement offices offer.

- The office has a list of job openings with local employers. After interviews with trained counselors, people who seem to be able to do a particular job are sent for **job interviews**. At these interviews, an employer often decides if they would be good to hire.

- People who want jobs in some trades can be placed in **apprenticeship programs**. In these programs people are trained while they work on the job. They gain practical experience under the supervision of skilled workers.

- People can get information about jobs available all over the country, not just in their city or state.

- If people are not sure what they can do or what they want to do, job counselors may give them tests to see what they do best and to learn more about their abilities and interests.

When Maria first talked to a counselor, she was a little uncomfortable answering so many personal questions. However, she knew that the counselor had to ask such questions because from her answers, the counselor could more easily match her with a job that suited her.

Counselor

A person at an employment agency or job placement office who helps another person find a job; a person who gives advice to someone else.

Job interview

A meeting during which the person doing the hiring asks questions and rates the answers of the person applying for a job.

Apprenticeship program

A work-training program.

Many job placement offices may also ask you to fill out an application. The steps in Chapter 4 of this book will help you do a good job filling out an application for a job. *(See pages 75–76.)*

Activity B   Number your paper 1 to 8. Then write short answers to these questions.

1) Where would you go to apply for work with the U.S. government?

2) Do you have to pay a fee at a city or state job placement office?

3) How do the job placement offices get their lists of available jobs?

4) Where can you find the telephone numbers of government placement offices?

5) Why do counselors interview people who want jobs?

6) What is an apprenticeship program?

7) Why might you want information about jobs available in other cities and states?

8) Why would a counselor give you a test?

Chapter Summary

In this chapter both you and Maria Rodriguez learned certain skills that are helpful when looking for a job. For example, you need to know how to read ads from the help-wanted section of the newspaper and how to understand what those ads mean. Then you need to decide if you can do the jobs that are being advertised.

Help-wanted ads are placed in alphabetical order, usually by the name of the job. Sometimes these ads use abbreviations to get a lot of information into a small space. Understanding those abbreviations will help you easily read the ads.

Then you must decide if you can do a certain job. Do you have the skills that the job requires—such as working with certain machinery or using certain tools? You also should think about whether or not this is a job you would like to do and whether or not the job would pay enough money to meet your needs.

In addition to using newspaper ads, you can also get a job through employment agencies and job placement offices. Employment agencies charge a fee for finding you a job, but job placement offices, which are city or state government offices, do not charge a fee.

Part A Review your understanding of ad abbreviations.

1) Rewrite these two ads, replacing the abbreviations with complete words.

a)

me	
' help	**DRIVER** Coll. stu. w/car. P/t, Tues. and Thurs. Must have good driving record. Refs. req. No exp. nec. Pos. avail. immed. Send letter of app. and refs. by fax to 555-7650.	locate bene. t help ou
.ind of rk. so Perm.		**CARETA** exp. nec good

b)

| it pos. eeded | **SALES** Exp'd. w/refs. High comm. Must be h.s. grad. F/t, eves. Good sal. Bene. incl. ins. Apply in pers. - 8900 Business Blvd | **TRAVEL** exp. nec good |
| r the ocate me | | **TRUCK** the loca |

2) Select an ad from the help-wanted section of your newspaper. Then rewrite it without using any abbreviations.

Part B Number your paper 1 to 20. Then rewrite these job titles in alphabetical order.

pediatric instructor
sales representative
auto mechanic
program analyst
cosmetic demonstrator
pediatric nurse
receptionist
purchasing agent
occupational therapist
clerk

construction supervisor
pediatric assistant
sales secretary
program manager
cosmetic sales
sales trainee
construction superintendent
purchasing manager
production coordinator
construction manager

ADMINISTRATIVE ASSISTANT
Should have exc. typ. skills & at least some exp. w/word processing prog. Grammar & math skills are req.—plus knowledge of comp. spreadsheets Exc. sal., bene. Call Sue at 555-0653 between 10 a.m. & noon, Mon & Tues.

Part C   Number your paper 1 to 5. Then after you read this ad, list five qualifications that a person would need to have to apply for this job.

Part D   Number your paper 1 to 10. Then write short answer to these questions.

1) Where can you find information about jobs that are available? List at least three ways to find a job.

2) What services are provided at city and state job placement offices? List at least four services.

3) What questions should you ask yourself to determine if you should apply for a particular job? List at least five questions.

4) What things should you know about an employment agency before you go there for help in finding a job?

5) In what part of the paper can you find ads for jobs?

6) In what order are these ads arranged?

7) What three things should you think about in order to decide if a job suits you?

8) Why do you think employers don't like to hire people who change jobs too often?

9) How can the Yellow Pages of the telephone directory help you to find a job?

10) If you were looking in the telephone directory for these three agencies, which would be listed first? Which would be listed second? Which would be listed last?

Barker Job Agency
Baker Job Agency
Berke Job Associates, Inc.

Test Taking Tip   After you have taken a test, go back and reread the questions and your answers. Ask yourself, "Do my answers show that I understood the question?"

FOR LOCAL POSTMARK

"FOR TODAYS POSTMARK"
MAIL MUST BE DEPOSITED
PRIOR TO 6:30 P.M.

MONDAY – FRIDAY

5:00PM ON SATURDAY

NONE ON SUNDAY

Chapter 2

Applying by Letter

Sometimes long before an employer ever gets to meet you in person, he or she will begin to judge you by the way you write a letter. If a letter you send doesn't make a good impression, you may never get your foot in the door—even if you qualify for the job.

In Chapter 2, you will not only learn the correct form for a business letter, but you will also find out what information to put in it.

Goals for Learning

▶ To understand the seven parts of a business letter and how to punctuate them correctly

▶ To be able to use either the full block style or the modified block style for a business letter

▶ To know what information to include in a letter of application

▶ To be able to address a business envelope correctly

▶ To be able to use the two-letter post office abbreviations for states in your letters and on your envelopes

When Aldo Carducci applied by letter for three jobs and didn't get interviewed for any of them, he was concerned. He went to his teacher at night school and asked her what he should do. After Mrs. Levy looked at copies of Aldo's letters, she had an idea why he hadn't gotten any of the jobs. She said to him, "If you learn how to write a good **letter of application**, your chances of getting a job will improve greatly. I believe it's possible that you didn't get any of the jobs because your letters not only didn't follow the correct form, but more importantly they didn't say the right things."

"How can I learn to write a letter that will get me a job?" Aldo asked.

"Come to class a half an hour early for the next few weeks, and I will give you some extra help," promised Mrs. Levy.

Because Aldo really needed a good job, he went early to Mrs. Levy's class every evening for three weeks. First, Aldo learned the parts of a business letter. Although business letters may differ some in form, they all have seven basic parts:

1. Return address
2. Date
3. Inside address
4. Salutation or greeting
5. Body
6. Complimentary close
7. Signature

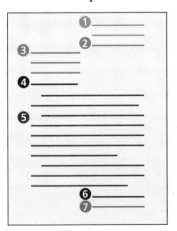

> **Letter of application**
>
> *A letter used in making a request to be hired.*

> **Return address**
>
> *The street address, city, state, and ZIP code of the person writing the letter.*

> **ZIP code**
>
> *The postal delivery area number written after the name of a state in an address.*

1. The **return address** begins with your house number and street name or apartment number and street address. On the next line, directly underneath, comes the city and state in which you live, plus your **ZIP code**. This number is used to identify postal delivery areas in the United States.

Body

The part of a letter that tells why the person wrote the letter.

Date

The month, day, and year used on a letter to tell when it was written.

Inside address

The complete name and address of the person or company receiving the letter.

Salutation

The greeting to the person receiving the letter; for example, Dear Ms. Evans: or Dear Sir:.

2. The **date** on which you write the letter should be written directly under your address. The return address and date should look like the following example. Notice that a comma goes between the city and state but not between the state and the ZIP code. A comma also goes between the day and the year.

1230 Girard Drive
Houston, TX 77044
November 24, 2001

3. The **inside address** includes the complete name and address of the person and/or the company where the letter will be sent—such as the following example. Again, notice that a comma goes between the city and the state but not between the state and the ZIP code.

Ms. Julia Evans
Division of Personnel
Landers Advertising Agency
1600 West South Street
Louisville, KY 40201

4. The **salutation** is a way of greeting the person to whom you are writing. In a business letter, the salutation should be formal—such as the following example. Notice that a salutation is followed by a colon.

Dear Ms. Evans:

5. The **body** of the letter tells why you are writing. Read the following example of a letter written in answer to a help-wanted ad.

I am replying to your advertisement for a cashier that appeared in *The Evening Chronicle.* I am a recent graduate of Samuel Jones High School. While I was in school, I helped to run the school store. I have over two years of experience in using a cash register.

In addition, I am good in math, and I know how to run several machines. I also like meeting people.

I would very much like to come in for an interview. Please call me at 555-3211.

Complimentary close

The polite ending to a letter; for example, Sincerely, *or* Respectfully yours,.

6. The **complimentary close** is a way of ending the letter politely. In a business letter, the complimentary close should be formal—such as the following example. Notice that it is followed by a comma.

Sincerely yours **,**

7. The **signature** tells the person receiving the letter who you are. Your signature should be neat and easy to read. In a business letter, it is common to include a handwritten signature above a printed full name—such as this example.

Signature

A handwritten (rather than typed or printed) name following the close in a letter; business letters often include a handwritten signature above the typed full name.

Aldo Carducci

Aldo Carducci

After Aldo had studied the parts of a business letter, Mrs. Levy gave him a test. See how well you understand the seven parts of a business letter.

Activity A   Number your paper 1 to 7. Then match the parts of a letter in the first column with the correct description in the second column. (See if you can do this activity without looking back in the book to find the answers.)

Parts of a Letter

1) return address

2) signature

3) salutation

4) date

5) complimentary close

6) inside address

7) body

Description

a) tells the person who you are

b) is a way of greeting the person to whom you are writing

c) has your address and the city and state where you live

d) tells why you are writing

e) includes the name and address of the person to whom you are writing

f) tells when the letter was written

g) is a polite way of closing your letter

Full block style

A form of business writing in which all the parts of a letter are written against the left margin; no paragraphs are indented.

Mrs. Levy told Aldo that most business letters use either the **full block style** or a variation of the block style. She gave him this diagram of the full block style so that he could see where the parts of the letter go on a page.

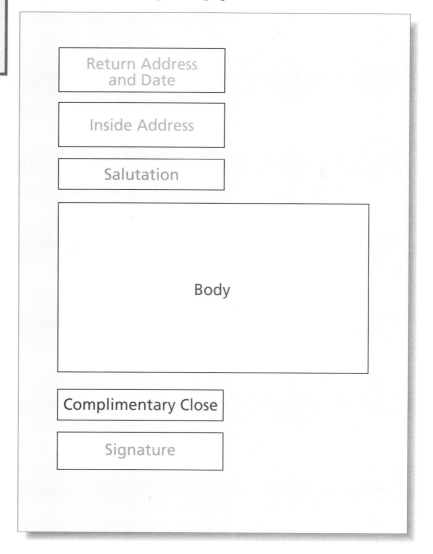

Return Address and Date

Inside Address

Salutation

Body

Complimentary Close

Signature

Next, Mrs. Levy showed Aldo a sample letter in full block style. Compare this letter with the diagram on the previous page.

4326 Arden Avenue
Houston, TX 77013
September 30, 2001

Ms. Esther Fine
Mighty Fine Company
4511 Leeds Road
Houston, TX 77019

Dear Ms. Fine:

I am writing in answer to your ad for a file clerk that appeared in last night's Daily Report.

I have worked at Bell, Inc., for three years as a file clerk and have always received very high ratings on my job performance. However, because Bell, Inc., is closing, I am looking for another position.

I would like to come in for an interview. I can be reached at 555-3255.

Yours very truly,

Lillian S. Levy

Lillian S. Levy

Margin

The outside edge of a page on which there is no writing or printing.

Aldo noticed that all seven parts of the letter were up against the left **margin**. He also noticed that the letter was carefully spaced with one blank line between each part of the letter and one blank line between each paragraph.

Activity A   Number your paper 1 to 7. Then write the correct name of the letter part next to each number.

5617 Kelly Street
Madison, WI 53701   **1**
April 5, 2001   **2**

Personnel Director
Clean Soap Company   **3**
2 East 33rd Street
Madison, WI 53702

Dear Personnel Director: **4**

I am writing to apply for the job of packer that was advertised at the Wisconsin Employment Placement Center.

I have had no experiences as a packer, but I learn quickly. I had a good record of attendance at Green Waters High where I just graduated. I was never late in four years of high school.   **5**

If you would be interested in interviewing me, I can be reached at 555-0008.

Very truly yours,   **6**

Fred Soames
7
Fred Soames

Activity B Write your own full block style letter in answer to this ad.

MAILROOM CLERK   Good rdg. skills. F/T Mon. thru Fri., 6 a.m. to 2:30 p.m. Apply by mail, Griner, Inc., 44 Court Square, (your city).

Modified block style

In this form of business letter, the return address, date, complimentary close, and signature are lined up near the center of the page; paragraphs are indented.

After Aldo had learned the full block style, Mrs. Levy said, "Now, Aldo, there's another form you should learn. It's called the **modified block style**."

Mrs. Levy then gave Aldo this diagram of the modified block style of the business letter for him to study.

Return Address and Date

Inside Address

Salutation

Body

Complimentary Close

Signature

Aldo remembered that he had a letter in his notebook. He showed it to Mrs. Levy and said. "Isn't this letter written in modified block style?"

Mrs. Levy looked at the letter and said, "Yes, you're absolutely right!"

This is what Aldo's letter looked like.

47 Winslow Drive
Cedar Rapids, IA 52401
December 12, 2001

Mr. Aldo Carducci
1230 Girard Drive
Houston, TX 77013

Dear Mr. Carducci:

    Thank you for ordering our special digital watch. This item has been so popular that it will be three weeks before we can send the watch you ordered.

    We hope this delay will not cause you any inconvenience. We know you will be glad you waited!

Sincerely,

Isabel Diaz

Isabel Diaz
Mail Order Division

Indented

Set in from the margin of the page.

Aldo noticed that several parts of the modified block style letter were **indented** and did not go against the margin. He also noticed that the return address, date, complimentary close, and signature were placed directly under one another. He saw that this letter was also carefully spaced with one blank line between each part of the letter and a blank line between each paragraph.

Activity A On your paper, rewrite these parts of a letter in their correct places for a modified block style letter.

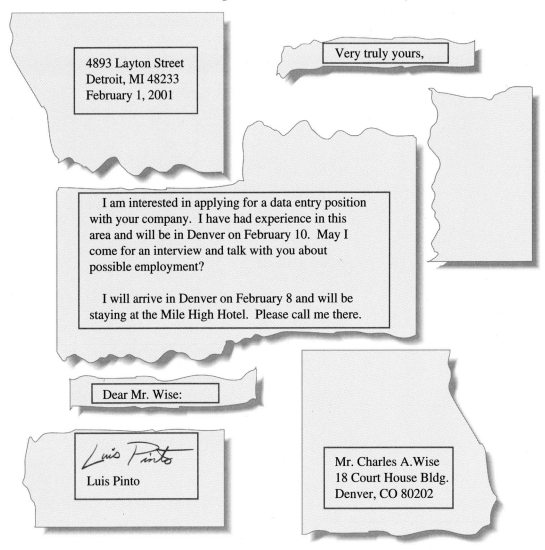

4893 Layton Street
Detroit, MI 48233
February 1, 2001

Very truly yours,

I am interested in applying for a data entry position with your company. I have had experience in this area and will be in Denver on February 10. May I come for an interview and talk with you about possible employment?

I will arrive in Denver on February 8 and will be staying at the Mile High Hotel. Please call me there.

Dear Mr. Wise:

Luis Pinto

Mr. Charles A. Wise
18 Court House Bldg.
Denver, CO 80202

Activity B On your paper, answer this ad in a letter that follows the modified block style.

SCHOOL CROSSING GUARD No exp. nec. Will train. Must be able to wk. Mon.-Fri. from 7:45 a.m. to 9:15 a.m. and from 2:30 p.m. to 3:30 p.m. Apply by letter to: Department of Transportation, 115 Main Street, (your city).

You have just studied two styles of business letters: full block and modified block. The following review activities will help you understand the differences between these two forms.

Activity A   On your paper, list the seven parts of a business letter in the order in which they should appear.

- inside address
- body
- return address
- signature
- date
- salutation
- complimentary close

Activity B   Number your paper 1 to 9. Then answer these questions about the full block style of a letter.

1) If you are writing a letter using full block style, where would you put your street address?

2) Where would you put your city, state, and ZIP code?

3) Where would you put the date?

4) Where would you put the name of the person to whom you are writing?

5) Should you indent each paragraph?

6) How many lines would you leave between each paragraph?

7) Where would you put the complimentary close?

8) Where would you put your signature?

9) Many people who use computers write their letters in the full block style because they say that it is easier and that they are less likely to make mistakes. Why do you think they feel this way?

Activity C   Number your paper 1 to 7. Then answer these questions about the modified block style of a letter.

1) If you are using the modified block style, where would you put your city, state, and ZIP code?

2) Where would you put the date?

3) Where would you put the name of the person to whom you are writing?

4) Should you indent each paragraph?

5) How many lines would you leave between each paragraph?

6) Where would you put the complimentary close?

7) Where would you put your signature?

Aldo carefully prepares his letter of application to make a good first impression.

"I've learned a lot about business letters," Aldo said to Mrs. Levy. "You've been a big help to me."

"We're not done yet," said Mrs. Levy. "After you know the correct form for a letter, you also need to learn about what goes into the body of a letter. It must contain the right information."

"What is the right information?" asked Aldo.

"The right information is all the information that the employer will need to know. Before you begin writing, plan what you will say. Then write your letter," Mrs. Levy said.

"But how will I know if I have written a good letter?" asked Aldo.

Mrs. Levy said, "Here is a list of five questions to ask yourself after you have written your letter. If you can answer Yes to all these questions, you have a good letter."

1. Have I identified the job title and told exactly how I found out about the job?

2. Have I listed the skills I have that would help me do the job?

References

People who can describe what you are like and what kind of a worker you would be.

3. Have I given **references** if they are asked for? References are names of people you know who can describe the kind of person you are, the things you do well, and/or the way you get along with others. Good references include friends, teachers, clergy, and past employers.

4. Have I given a telephone number where I can be reached if a person from the company wants to contact me?

5. Have I told the person at the company what time I can be reached at this phone number?

"And don't forget to check your finished letter for correct spelling, punctuation, and capitalization," Mrs. Levy said. "An employer will be looking for that!"

Activity A Number your paper 1 to 5. Then after you read the body of this letter of application, ask the five questions listed on page 31. If you can answer Yes to the question, write *Yes* next to the number. Otherwise, write *No*.

I read your ad for a job. I am interested in applying for this position.

I know the major word processing programs and have good English skills. I graduated from high school. I am 28 years old. My birthday is August 30.

Following are my references:
Mr. John Hammond, owner
John's Car Wash
1518 Fulton Street
Baton Rouge, LA 70821

Ms. Myra Green, teacher
Lockland High School
4000 Mars Drive
Baton Rouge, LA 70824

If you would like me to come in for an interview, call me between 7:00 A.M. and 9:00 A.M. or after 5:00 P.M.

Knowing What to Leave Out

"It is just as important to know what to leave out of a letter of application as it is to know what to put in," Mrs. Levy explained. "Employers don't want to read letters full of information that has nothing to do with the job!" In the body of the letter on page 32, there are two pieces of information that should have been left out: the age of the person writing and the person's birthday.

Aldo thought carefully and then asked, "How do I know what to leave out?"

"Provide only the information asked for in the ad or in the job summary at the agency or placement office," Mrs. Levy replied, "and don't worry about anything else."

Activity B   Number your paper 1 to 10. Then decide which of the following facts you should include in a letter answering this ad. Write *Yes* or *No* for each answer.

PRINTER'S ASST.
h.s. grad w/exp. Have good attend. rec. Apply by letter to Good Printing Co., 487 Oak Lane, (your city).

Fact List

1) Word processing skills

2) Whether you have a driver's license

3) Whether you graduated from high school

4) Your high school grades

5) Two references

6) Your good history grades

7) The award you got for perfect attendance

8) Your part-time job as a printer's helper

9) The distance between your house and the company advertising the job

10) Your telephone number

Activity C Number your paper 1 to 5. Then decide which of the following facts you should include in a letter answering this ad. Write *Yes* or *No* for each answer.

BOOKKEEPER Some exp. pref. Must be good in math. Driv. lic. helpful Apply by letter. Morgan Bros., 27 Lee Ave., (your city).

Fact List

1) Your good math grades

2) Your poor physical education grades

3) Your experience in helping your father keep his books

4) The time it will take you to get to work

5) That you have a new car

Activity D On your paper, list the information that you would include if you wrote a letter of application for each of these jobs.

1) You are writing to apply for the job of cabinet maker. The company wants a person with experience and a good attendance record. It wants someone who has served as an apprentice in cabinet making and knows how to use all the tools. You think you can handle this job. What information would you include in your letter of application?

2) You are writing to apply for the job of nurse's assistant in a hospital. The ad states that the hospital wants someone who has worked in a hospital before and who has experience in working with patients. It also wants someone who can work odd hours. You think you would like this job. What information would you include in your letter of application?

"The best way to become a good letter writer is to practice," advised Mrs. Levy.

"But writing letters is hard work," Aldo said with a sigh.

"That's true," said Mrs. Levy, "but the more letters you write, the easier it will get. You'll begin to see which kinds of sentences sound good and which kinds don't. You'll begin to remember what should be included in each letter. Besides, when you get a good job, all that hard work will have been worth it!"

Mrs. Levy is right. The letter you send to someone is a part of you. The person judges you from the way the letter looks and the way it sounds. If you want to make a good impression, work hard and practice your skills. Then when someone looks at your letter, that person will think, "This is someone I would like to hire."

Activity A Read this help-wanted ad. Then write the body of the letter that you would write to apply for this job.

> **SALES TRAINEE** for ins. co. No exp. nec. Should have good math and English skills. Answer by letter including 2 refs. to McGill Company, 904 Glenn Drive, (your city).

Activity B Read this next help-wanted ad. Write a complete letter answering the ad. Use full block or modified block style. Be sure to include the seven parts of a business letter.

> **SHIPPING CLERK** for nat'l. co. Must be h.s. grad. No exp. nec. Should have good org. skills. Apply by let. to Tamara Kirk, K. L. Auto Parts, 3281 Fernwood Road, (your city).

Aldo practiced writing letters of application, using both the full block and the modified block style. Then Mrs. Levy said, "Aldo, there's one last thing you need to know about letters—the proper way to address an envelope." Then she added, "After all of your hard work, you want to make sure that your letter gets to where it is supposed to go!"

This is the sample envelope Mrs. Levy showed Aldo.

Ms. Ella Black
112 South Central Street
Cheyenne, WY 82001

Brown, Ellis, and Company
8832 Louden Avenue
Pittsburgh, PA 15219

Notice that the return address, which is in the upper left-hand corner of the envelope, includes the person who sent the letter. On the second line is the street address, and directly under that is the city, state, and ZIP code—all on the same line.

Notice also that the name and address of the person and/or the company receiving the letter is several lines under the return address and considerably to the right. This arrangement gives the envelope a balanced look. The stamp, of course, goes in the upper right-hand corner.

Remember to include the ZIP code on every letter you send. Leaving it out may delay your letter considerably. If you don't know someone's ZIP code, you can look it up in a ZIP code book at a post office or a library.

Activity A On your paper, draw an envelope measuring $9\frac{1}{2}$ inches from left to right and 4 inches up and down. Then use this information to address the envelope.

> This letter is being sent by Joseph Hall. Mr. Hall lives at 6715 Hartsfield Road in Baltimore, MD. His ZIP code is 21218. The letter is being sent to Hans Olsen. Mr. Olsen lives at 13 North Lanier Place in Trenton, NJ. His ZIP code is 08608.

Activity B Select from the newspaper a help-wanted ad that must be answered by letter. Tape the ad to the top of your paper. Then draw another $9\frac{1}{2} \times 4''$ envelope and address it, using the information in the ad. (Use your own return address.)

Lesson 8 Abbreviations for State Names

Post office abbreviations

Two-letter state abbreviations that do not include periods.

Mrs. Levy handed Aldo a list of state abbreviations and said, "You will use this list a lot because these two-letter **post office abbreviations** are commonly used both on the envelope and on the inside addresses of a letter. These short abbreviations help to keep the city, state, and ZIP code all on one line. Notice that both letters in the post office abbreviations are capitals without any periods."

"The two-letter postal abbreviations for the states are not always formed in the same way," explained Mrs. Levy. "For example, the abbreviation for Alabama (AL) uses the first and second letters of the state name, while the abbreviation for Alaska (AK) uses the first and fifth letters of the state name. Because of this, it is difficult to remember all of the abbreviations. This list will help you."

"Thank you," said Aldo. "I'll keep this list handy in my notebook," Aldo said.

Activity A   Copy this list of state abbreviations that Mrs. Levy gave to Aldo. Then put your copy in a safe place so that you can always find it.

Alabama	AL	Montana	MT
Alaska	AK	Nebraska	NE
Arizona	AZ	Nevada	NV
Arkansas	AR	New Hampshire	NH
California	CA	New Jersey	NJ
Colorado	CO	New Mexico	NM
Connecticut	CT	New York	NY
Delaware	DE	North Carolina	NC
District of Columbia	DC	North Dakota	ND
Florida	FL	Ohio	OH
Georgia	GA	Oklahoma	OK
Hawaii	HI	Oregon	OR
Idaho	ID	Pennsylvania	PA
Illinois	IL	Rhode Island	RI
Indiana	IN	South Carolina	SC
Iowa	IA	South Dakota	SD
Kansas	KS	Tennessee	TN
Kentucky	KY	Texas	TX
Louisiana	LA	Utah	UT
Maine	ME	Vermont	VT
Maryland	MD	Virginia	VA
Massachusetts	MA	Washington	WA
Michigan	MI	West Virginia	WV
Minnesota	MN	Wisconsin	WI
Mississippi	MS	Wyoming	WY
Missouri	MO		

Activity B   Draw a $9\frac{1}{2} \times 4''$ envelope. Then address the envelope with this information.

This letter is being sent by Maria Gonzalez. Ms. Gonzalez lives at 202 Adams Street in Detroit, Michigan. Her ZIP code is 48238. The letter is being sent to Rose Chang. Ms. Chang lives at 45 South Elm Place in Houston, Texas. Her ZIP code is 77015.

Mrs. Levy and Aldo had worked through all the steps he needed to know about writing a letter of application. Now he was on his own, but he felt confident because he had studied and worked hard.

When Aldo got ready to write a real letter of application, he made a list of the things that Mrs. Levy had taught him. Here's that list.

1. Use a correct form for a business letter. The two forms used most often are the full block style and the modified block style.

   a. **Full Block Style**   All seven parts of the business letter go up against the left-hand margin.

   b. **Modified Block Style**   The return address, the date, each paragraph, the complimentary close, and the signature are indented.

2. The body of the letter should include all the information requested in the ad. It should also include a telephone number and the times you can be reached.

3. No matter which style of letter you use, the envelope should have the return address in the upper left-hand corner. The address of the person to whom you're writing should be several lines below that and toward the center. The stamp goes in the upper right-hand corner. (See an example of an envelope on page 36.)

4. Use the two-letter post office abbreviations on the envelope and in the addresses on the inside of a letter. Remember, these abbreviations do not have any periods.

Part A Number your paper 1 to 10. If the statement is true, write *True* next to the number. If it is not true, write *False*.

1) The parts of a business letter are the return address, inside address, salutation, body, and complimentary close.

2) A letter should always include the date on which the letter is written.

3) The salutation is a way of greeting the person you're writing to.

4) The body of the letter tells why you are writing.

5) In the full block style letter, everything except the body of the letter lines up at the right-hand margin.

6) The modified block style letter has indented paragraphs.

7) You don't have to give references if you don't want to include them.

8) Unless a company asks for your telephone number, don't include it in your letter.

9) When you write a letter of application, it is a good idea to list all of your hobbies.

10) Always include a return address on an envelope.

Part B Rewrite this list of the seven parts of a business letter in the order in which they should appear in a letter.

- body
- date
- signature
- return address
- complimentary close
- inside address
- salutation

Part C   Read this full block style letter that contains mistakes and leaves out important information. Then after you write the numbers of the lines that need to be improved, explain each mistake. Remember, incorrect punctuation would be considered a mistake.

1)	2517 Bartley Street
2)	Chicago, Ill. 60609
3)	September 12, 2001
4)	Dr. Phillip Moore
5)	12 Arrington Circle
6)	Miami, FL
7)	Dear Mr. Moore
8)	I saw your ad in the *Chicago Flash* for a
9)	receptionist. I will be moving to Miami next
10)	month. I am interested in applying for the job.
11)	I have worked as a receptionist for a doctor
12)	here in Chicago for four years. I like meeting
13)	and working with people
14)	If you would like an interview, please call
15)	me when I get to Miami.
16)	Love
17)	
18)	Cynthia

Part D   Rewrite the letter in Part C. Correct all of the errors and add any information you think is necessary for a good letter of application. When you finish, address an envelope for this letter.

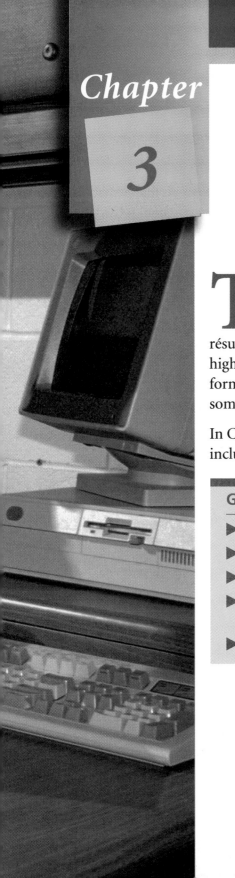

Chapter 3

Including a Résumé

To get a job that you really want, you have to make yourself stand out from all of the other people applying for the same job. One way to do that is to submit a résumé along with a job application. Because a résumé highlights important information about you in an easy-to-read format, your application is more likely to get attention than someone else's application that did not include a résumé.

In Chapter 3, you will learn what information you should include on a résumé and how to organize the information.

Goals for Learning

▶ To understand the advantages of a résumé

▶ To know what information to include on a résumé

▶ To know how to organize the information on a résumé

▶ To learn the differences between a résumé for a recent high school graduate and an experienced worker

▶ To write your own résumé and to be able to make it perfect

Tyron Williams went to see an employment counselor at his state's job placement office. He had not been able to get the type of job he had wanted even though he had been trying since he got out of high school three months before.

When Ms. Drake interviewed Tyron, she realized that he had many good points in his favor. He had a good school record and had worked part time. His references from his part-time job were excellent. Tyron also was personable and polite, and he seemed to know how to apply for a job both in person and by letter. After Ms. Drake asked more questions, she thought she knew what Tyron might have been missing.

"Perhaps," she said, "no employer has gotten a real picture of your ability. If you had included a **résumé** with your letters or had taken one with you to your interviews, you might have gotten a job before now."

"How could a résumé have helped me?" asked Tyron.

"Only so many facts can or should be told in a letter of application," Ms. Drake answered, "but a résumé can give a clearer picture of you and your qualifications. It gives you a chance to tell an employer important additional information in an easy-to-read style."

"I learned to write a résumé in high school," Tyron said. "If I go back and look over my notes, I think I could write a good description of my skills." Then he asked Ms. Drake, "After I write my résumé, will you look it over?"

"Of course, I will," she said with a smile. "As soon as you have finished writing your résumé, call and make an appointment to come in and see me."

Résumé

A summary of one's career and qualifications that is used when a person is applying for a job.

Among his notes at home, Tyron found a list of reasons why a person should submit a résumé with every job application. Here is that list.

1. A résumé gives you a chance to present yourself in a positive manner.

2. You can give more information about yourself in a résumé than it is possible to give in a letter or even on some applications.

3. A good résumé will show an employer how well you can organize information.

4. A résumé tells the employer that you really care about getting the job because you have taken the time and trouble to write a résumé.

The four points on this list made sense to Tyron. He remembered having come away from job interviews thinking, "I wish I had been asked about my attendance record at school or my math grades." He also had wished that he could have told more about himself on job applications.

Activity A Follow these tips to begin creating your résumé.

Put your mind to work. What information should you include on your résumé? Think of some of the important things about yourself that you would like an employer to know. Have you had any jobs? Did you do well in certain subjects in school? Have you won any awards? Are there some **business machines** that you know how to operate? For example, have you ever used a computer, a fax, or a copier? Who would you list as references?

Business machines

Equipment used by most companies.

On a piece of paper, write down everything you can think of that you would like to include on your résumé. Then keep this list in your notebook to use later in this chapter.

As Tyron looked over his notes, he remembered that a résumé has several important parts that include specific information. This is what he had written in his notes.

A résumé should include the following parts:

- Personal information
- Career objectives
- Education
- Employment experience
- Extracurricular and community activities
- Awards and honors
- References

Order

The placing of topics or events in a reasonable arrangement; the order could be by time, importance, space, cost, etc.

Personal information should always come first in a résumé. After that, the arrangement or **order** of these parts should most often be decided by your age, your experience, and the job for which you are applying. Generally, however, the most important information is listed near the beginning of a résumé.

Although you are not required to give your age on a résumé, it does play a role in what you have done and what you are qualified to do. Extracurricular activities are also valuable for recent graduates to include on a résumé. However, if you have been out of high school for awhile, you probably shouldn't list any. Instead, you could list your membership in community groups or activities in which you participate.

If you are a recent graduate, you probably will have little or no work experience. As a result, you shouldn't put this section at the top of your résumé. On the other hand, people who have had several jobs should put the employment section near the top of their résumé to show that they have had experience and are qualified for a new job.

Activity A   Number your paper 1 to 14. Then write the correct answer from the box that completes each statement. (Use each answer only once.)

employment	references	objectives
awards	order	community
graduated	information	age
seven	end	applying
résumé	experience	

There are **1)** _____ parts to a résumé. These parts include the following: personal **2)** _____ , career **3)** _____ , education, employment experience, extracurricular and community activities, **4)** _____ and honors, and **5)** _____ .

No definite **6)** _____ must be used when writing a résumé. The order should be decided by your **7)** _____ , your **8)** _____ , and the job for which you are **9)** _____ .

Extracurricular activities would be important for someone who has just **10)** _____ from high school. For people who have been out of high school for a while, it would be better to list **11)** _____ activities.

A person who has had no job experience either would not put the **12)** _____ section in the résumé at all or else would put this section near the **13)** _____ of his or her résumé. Someone who has previous job experience would probably list this information near the beginning of the **14)** _____ .

Tyron helps at the community center by coaching young basketball players.

Personal Information

Personal information includes your name, address, and telephone number. Also, be sure to include your ZIP code with your address and your area code with your telephone number. (Put parentheses around your area code.) This section should always come first on your résumé.

Career Objectives

Although you should word your **career objectives** and goals to fit the specific job that you want, you should make them broad enough so that you could be considered for more than one job. For example, if you are looking for a job as a plumbing trainee or apprentice, your long-range objective might be "to become a master plumber." Even though this objective would take you many years to achieve, it is still a worthy goal to pursue.

Education

For someone who has recently graduated from school, this section can be especially important on your résumé. Be sure to include special courses you have taken that relate to the job you are seeking. You should also mention areas or courses in which you got good grades.

Employment Experience

Work **experience** should include all full-time and part-time jobs that you have had. This section should also include any jobs you performed as a volunteer—such as baby-sitting, snow shoveling, lawn mowing, or other similar jobs done for neighbors or friends. Such experience will show that you are responsible and dependable and have initiative.

Extracurricular and Community Activities, Awards, and Honors

Recent high school graduates should include any **extracurricular** activities—activities beyond the regular school curriculum, such as participation in sports, the school newspaper, the band, and student government. All applicants should also include any community groups or activities in which they take part—such as offices held, specific duties performed, and awards earned. Employers often feel that people who are active in clubs and organizations will be hardworking and dependable on the job as well.

References

Include at least three references on your résumé. Relatives, of course, are not good choices for references. Employers think that relatives will say nice things about you just because you are related to them. Instead, references should be former employers, clergy, coaches, club sponsors, teachers, neighbors, and other adults who know you. Anyone you choose as a reference should be able to describe what your character is like, how well you do things, and how well you get along with others. You also should get permission from your references before putting their names on your résumé. Keep in mind that by law, previous employers can discuss only job-related issues when giving a reference.

Playing on a sports team is one extracurricular activity Tyron can put on his résumé.

Activity B On a piece of paper, draw a chart like the following one. Then after you read the list of information about Tyron Williams, write the number of each item in the correct column on your chart.

Personal Information	Objectives	Education	Experience	Extracurricular/ Community Activities

Information About Tyron Williams

1) Wants to be a licensed automobile mechanic

2) Sang in a school chorus

3) Graduated from high school

4) Worked part time in a gas station

5) Lives at 511 North Marine Street

6) Took an advanced course in auto mechanics at night school

7) Played on a community basketball team

8) Helped neighbors fix their cars

9) Would like to own his own auto repair shop

10) Took auto mechanics courses in high school

11) Lives in Walla Walla, WA 98511

12) Was treasurer of the high school shop club

13) Was a high school student government representative

14) Worked on weekends at AA Appliance Repair Shop

15) Has the following telephone number: (509) 555-7760

Rough draft

The first copy of a piece of writing; that piece will be revised, proofread, and corrected before a final copy is made.

Tyron Williams compiled the information he needed for his résumé by listing personal information plus facts about his career objectives, education, experience, extracurricular and community activities, and references. Then he was ready to write the first version, or **rough draft**, of his résumé.

Tyron prepares a rough draft of his résumé to organize his thoughts before he begins editing and revising the final version.

On the next page is a copy of the rough draft of Tyron's résumé. As you read it, find the main parts of the résumé. Also notice the information that he included in each part. Be prepared to answer questions about his résumé after you have studied it.

Tyron J. Williams
511 North Marine Street
Walla Walla, Washington 98511
(509) 555-7760

CAREER OBJECTIVES
- To be a licensed automobile mechanic
- To own my own auto repair shop

EDUCATION
- Graduated from Northwest High School, June, 2000
- Majored in auto mechanics
- Received best grades in math, science, and auto mechanics (B's)
- Completed advanced course in auto mechanics at Adult Night Center, June, 2001

EXTRACURRICULAR ACTIVITIES
- Treasurer of Shop Club
- Student government representative
- Member of the school chorus

EXPERIENCE
- Worked part time at Steiner's Service Station for two years
- Worked on Saturdays during senior year at AA Appliance Repair Shop
- Helped neighbors with car repairs

REFERENCES

Mr. Jacob Steiner, owner
Steiner's Service Station
11 Pacific Highway
Walla Walla, WA 98503
(509) 555-1742

Mr. William Turner,
auto mechanics teacher
Northwest High School
Walla Walla, WA 98513
(509) 555-6756

Mrs. Jeannette Robinson, neighbor
5155 North Marine Street
Walla Walla, WA 98511
(509) 555-9443

Activity A   Number your paper 1 to 10. Then answer these questions about Tyron Williams's résumé.

1) What education did Tyron list that relates to the job of automobile mechanic?

2) Why would an employer be impressed by Tyron's extracurricular activities?

3) Which two of Tyron's work experiences relate most directly to the job of auto mechanic?

4) Why is Mr. William Turner a good reference if Tyron is applying for a job as an auto mechanic?

5) Mrs. Robinson is one of the neighbors for whom Tyron has done car repairs. Why is she a good person for him to use as a reference?

6) Why do you think an employer would be especially impressed by Tyron's going to night school?

7) Why is Mr. Jacob Steiner a good reference?

8) How do Tyron's career objectives relate to the job of mechanic's assistant?

9) If you were thinking of hiring Tyron, which reference would you call first? Why?

10) What questions would you ask Mr. Steiner or Mr. Turner to get information that is not included on the résumé?

A Sample Résumé for an Experienced Person

Among his high school notes, Tyron found a sample résumé for an experienced job applicant. Because he couldn't use that sample to help him with his own résumé, he loaned it to Norman Flynn, a neighbor who wanted a new job.

Mr. Flynn still had a copy of his old résumé, which he had written 12 years before when he had graduated from high school. However, he quickly realized that he couldn't use it any longer for two reasons. First, the information on it was out of date. Second, he had gained more work experience that wasn't included on it. Norman also wanted to change the order of his résumé to emphasize different parts of it. Here is the new résumé that he wrote.

Norman H. Flynn
510 North Marine Street
Walla Walla, Washington 98511
(509) 555-2233

CAREER OBJECTIVE

- To be head bookkeeper for a large corporation

EXPERIENCE

2000 to present:	Assistant Bookkeeper Elgin's Department Store Walla Walla, WA 98546
1996 to 2000:	Bookkeeper Trainee Link's Hardware Stores Walla Walla, WA 98530
1999 to present:	Income Tax Consultant, part-time position Fill out income tax forms for 20 clients in spare time

COMMUNITY ACTIVITIES

2000 to present: Treasurer, Church of St. Jude

1999 to present: Treasurer and Business Manager,
Walla Walla Little League

1998 to present: Member, South Shores Community Group

1998 to present: Volunteer, South Shores General Hospital
Keep gift shop books

EDUCATION

June 1997:   Graduated from South Shores High

1997 to 1995:   Completed undergraduate courses at
Washington University in bookkeeping,
accounting, and computers

REFERENCES

Mr. Arthur Day, present employer   Rev. Julius Fitz, pastor
Elgin's Department Store   Church of St. Jude
3468 Main Street   7819 Wells Avenue
Walla Walla, WA 98546   Walla Walla, WA 98511
(509) 555-6983   (509) 555-4635

Mr. Felix Wist, president
South Shores General Hospital Volunteers
44 Hospital Road
Walla Walla, WA 98545
(509) 555-1297

How Mr. Flynn's Résumé Is Different

Notice the differences between the résumé Tyron Williams wrote and the one Mr. Flynn wrote. For example, the information on these two résumés is arranged differently to reflect the differences in age and experience of the two writers. There are also some important differences in the employment section and in the references section. Notice that Mr. Flynn was able to include more specific information in these two parts of his résumé.

Employment Experience

Mr. Flynn listed his work experience second in his résumé because he felt that information would be most interesting to an employer. He put community activities next because his activities in his community relate to accounting, the kind of work he is looking for.

References

Notice what a good selection of references Mr. Flynn made. First, he listed the man he now works for. A prospective employer would know that Mr. Flynn is being very open about the job he is presently doing.

Then Mr. Flynn listed the pastor of his church. The pastor could tell an employer about Mr. Flynn's character and also about the **volunteer** work he does as church treasurer.

Volunteer

One who provides a service freely and without being paid.

Finally, he listed the president of the volunteer group that he belongs to. This person could tell an employer about Mr. Flynn's volunteer work keeping the books for this organization.

Lesson 4 — Checklist for Résumés

Tyron found among his papers a list of capitalization, punctuation, and spelling rules that apply to résumés. Across the top of the list was this sentence written in big letters: *A RÉSUMÉ MUST BE PERFECT!*

Tyron was glad he found the list because it reminded him of the little things that can be very important when an employer looks at a résumé.

This is Tyron's list.

A RÉSUMÉ MUST BE PERFECT!

1. When writing an address, put a comma between the city and state. No punctuation goes between the state and the ZIP code. Use the two-letter state abbreviations, listed on page 38, for all addresses. Do not use a period after these abbreviations.

2. When writing a telephone number, put the area code in parentheses. Put a hyphen after the first three numbers of the telephone number.

3. Use capital letters for the first letter of all people's names, and names of streets, cities, states, businesses, schools, etc.

4. Spell all words correctly. Have someone else check the spelling on your résumé before you make a final copy.

Activity A   Number your paper 1 to 10. Then correct any résumé items that have errors. (There is a total of 12 errors.)

1) Oklahoma City, OK, 73125

2) Mr. John A fisher, Manager

3) 2634 Green Street

4) Mark Twain senior High school

5) February 14 1973

6) Mrs. Charlotte Best, Teacher

7) 301/555/4736

8) Bill's Discount store

9) Pennsylvania University

10) Dr Sylvia Greer

Activity B   On your own paper, list the items that you would include on your résumé.

• perfect attendance award two years in a row

• experience working at a full-time or part-time job

• activities in which you have participated at your church

• community groups to which you have belonged

• special courses you took in high school

Activity C On your paper, write the first draft of your own résumé. First, review the sample résumés in this section. Second, begin with the list of information you made in Activity A, page 45, and then add any additional information. Third, after you write your rough draft, use the following **checklist**. Finally, use a computer or typewriter to write a final draft.

Tyron chooses to copy his résumé onto nice paper he purchased at a copy shop.

Résumé Checklist

1. Have I chosen the best résumé order for my age and my experience?

2. Have I worded my career objectives so that they match the job that I want?

3. Have I listed all of my education—including any additional courses? Have I emphasized the things I did well in school? Have I highlighted courses that relate to the job I want?

4. If I have work experience, have I listed the specific skills and duties related to the job that I want?

5. Have I listed extracurricular activities and/or community activities that show my interest in areas related to the job I want?

6. Have I selected the most impressive references from all of the people who know me? Have I included the correct spelling of their names? Have I included their correct addresses and telephone numbers?

7. Are the headings clear? Do they stand out on the page?

8. Is all my information correct?

9. Is my wording consistent?

10. Have I corrected all spelling errors and typing errors?

11. Have I corrected all errors in capitalization and punctuation? Is my résumé perfect?

12. Have I followed all of the suggestions and the checklists in this chapter?

13. Did I center my name, address, and phone number at the top of the page? Is the rest of my résumé spaced well?

14. Have I been able to keep my résumé on one page—and definitely not more than two pages?

15. Is my final printed or typed copy neat and attractive?

A résumé is a valuable tool when you are looking for a job. It allows you to present more information about yourself than you could include in a letter or even a job application. A résumé gives an employer a better idea of what you can do.

A résumé should include personal information, career objectives, educational background, employment background, extracurricular and/or community activities, awards and honors, and references. How you arrange this information on a résumé depends on your age, the amount of experience you have had, and the information most important for the employer to know.

Probably the most important thing for you to remember about a résumé is that it should be perfect! It should be free of all errors in capitalization, punctuation, and spelling. All information—such as names, addresses, ZIP codes, and telephone numbers—must be correct.

A good résumé can make all the difference between being unemployed and getting a job or between getting a good job and getting a great job.

Part A   Number your paper 1 to 10. Then match each term in the first column with its description or definition in the second column.

Term

1) personal information
2) career objectives
3) education
4) employment experience
5) extracurricular activities
6) résumé
7) awards and honors
8) references
9) volunteer
10) community activities

Description

a) all full-time and part-time jobs you had
b) the names, addresses, and phone numbers of people who can describe your ability to do the job
c) what schools you graduated from; what courses you have taken
d) your name, address, and telephone number
e) school clubs and other high school activities you joined
f) a summary of one's qualifications for a job
g) special recognitions of your achievements
h) what you hope to be doing in the future
i) organizations you joined outside of school
j) one who provides a service without being paid

Part B   Number your paper 1 to 5. If the statement is true, write *True* next to the number. If it is not true, write *False*.

1) A recent high school graduate should probably list work experience before education.
2) The order of the items in a résumé should depend upon the job that the person wants.
3) You may leave your address and phone number out of your résumé.
4) An experienced person should probably list work experiences near the beginning of a résumé.
5) You can use your mother and father as references.

Part C   On a piece of paper, rewrite this part of a résumé, making all necessary corrections.

willaim t rogers
1758 maple streat
philadelphia pennsylvania, 19032
215 555 8493

referances

mr john dilland owner
dilland corner store
788 cherry lane
philadelphia pennsylvania 19024
215/555/4466

eduction

graduated from central high school,
june 2001
took courses in english and math
at pennsylvania state college

Part D   Number your paper 1 to 5. Then write short answers to these questions.

1) Why should you include a résumé with a letter of application?

2) What are the main parts of a résumé?

3) How would you decide the order of the sections of your résumé?

4) What kind of information should you include in the section for extracurricular and community activities?

5) Should you include as a reference a boss with whom you could not get along? Why or why not?

Test Taking Tip   Before you begin a test, look over it quickly. Try to set aside enough time to complete each section.

Filling Out an Application

O ften an employer will make a judgment about you long before you ever put a foot inside the front door of the company. In fact, you may be rejected for a job without ever meeting a single person in the company. How well you fill out an application might determine whether you are accepted or rejected for a job.

In Chapter 4, you will learn how to make an application represent you positively.

Goals for Learning

▶ To write a fact sheet that contains information needed on job applications

▶ To understand why fact sheets should be updated from time to time

▶ To understand vocabulary that commonly appears on job applications

▶ To be able to fill out job applications thoroughly and completely

Job application

A form used in making a request to be hired.

Supervisor

Someone who is in charge of others; a boss.

Yolanda Medina worked as an administrative assistant in the personnel department of Caine Supply Company. Every day she saw people come in to apply for jobs, and every day she saw some of their **job applications** thrown into the wastebasket. Because this practice puzzled her, she asked her **supervisor**, "Why do so many job applications get thrown out?"

Her supervisor explained, "If applications have mistakes in them or if all the information is not filled in, we simply don't bother with them. Why consider someone with a sloppy, careless application when we can hire someone with a completed application?" She added, "We think that the way people fill out an application is a sign of what kind of employee they might be. A carefully filled out application could indicate a thoughtful, hard-working employee."

A few weeks after Yolanda's talk with her supervisor, her younger brother Carlos graduated from high school. Already he was looking for a job. Yolanda told him about what her supervisor had said and warned him to do a good job filling out any job applications.

After several weeks went by and Carlos still did not have a job, Yolanda asked him why he was having trouble.

"I don't know, Yolanda," he said. "I bet I've filled out 20 applications, and still no job! I'm filling out another application to turn in this afternoon."

"Let me take a look at it," said Yolanda. She didn't have to look long before she shook her head and said, "No wonder you're not getting a job. This application has mistakes in it, you left out information, and you made sloppy corrections." She put her arm around her brother's shoulders and said, "Don't you remember my telling you that employers judge people by their applications? If they don't like what they see, they won't interview you."

"I guess I forgot," replied Carlos. "How about some help?"

Social Security number

A nine-digit number used to identify Americans for government purposes relating to taxes, unemployment payments, old-age and survivor benefits, and so on.

"First," said Yolanda, "I suggest you prepare a **fact sheet** with all the information you have to put on an application. Then take the fact sheet with you when you apply for a job. It's especially helpful if you have to fill out an application at the company's personnel office. Even if you fill out an application at home, the fact sheet is useful because all the information you need is in one place!"

"What would I put on a fact sheet?" Carlos asked.

"What information have you needed most often for those other 20 applications?" questioned Yolanda.

"You mean information like my **Social Security number** and my **school records**?" asked Carlos.

"Exactly," said Yolanda. "Look at my fact sheet."

This is the fact sheet that Yolanda gave her brother to use.

FACT SHEET

Social Security Number: 777-38-0976

EDUCATION

John Murphy Senior High 1600 McNair Avenue Topeka, Kansas 66656	Course: Business Years attended: 4 Graduated: June 2, 1998
Topeka Community College 203 South Plains Road Topeka, Kansas 66623	Course: Computer Programming Years attended: 2 Graduated: June 4, 2000 Degree: Associate of Arts

EXPERIENCE

1998 to present: Caine Supply Company 1543 Travis Street Topeka, Kansas 66609 (913) 555-1758	Position: Administrative Assistant Supervisor: Timothy Clark Reason for leaving: To get job as computer programmer

REFERENCES

Ms. Amelia Carter Business Education Teacher John Murphy Senior High (See above for address) (913) 555-0770	Ms. Lillian Newly Programming Instructor Topeka Community College (See above for address) (913) 555-9063

Mr. Timothy Clark, President
Caine Supply Company
(See above for address)
(913) 555-7718

As Carlos looked over his sister's fact sheet, he could see why she had included the information she did. He remembered that when he was filling out an application one day, he was so nervous that he forgot his Social Security number. Because he hadn't brought his card with him, he had to leave that space blank. He also remembered not being sure how long he had worked at a part-time job he had had in high school. He also remembered guessing at the spelling of several important names.

Later that evening Yolanda gave him a few helpful hints. "If you don't remember how to spell people's names, call and ask. The people won't mind. If you are not sure how to spell street or business names, look them up in the telephone book and check the spelling."

Activity A   Number your paper 1 to 10. Then write *Yes* for the items that you should include on your fact sheet. Write *No* for the items that you should not include.

1) The full name of the high school you attended

2) Your Social Security number

3) The number of basketball games in which you scored more than five points

4) The name of a teacher who was very nice to you—even though you were never in one of her classes

5) The address and ZIP code of the high school you attended

6) The name and address of your favorite aunt (as a reference)

7) The name of the company where you work

8) The name and address of the math teacher you had last year (as a reference)

9) The name of the principal of your school (as a reference)

10) The reason you want to leave your present job

Activity B   Write your own fact sheet. Include all of the information that Yolanda included on hers. Then add any additional information you might need on a job application. (Use the hints that Yolanda gave her brother.)

Updating Your Fact Sheet

From time to time you will have to update your fact sheet in order to include new jobs or any additional education. In fact, each time you apply for a job, you should check your fact sheet to make sure that all the information on it is current.

Activity C   On a piece of paper, list the names of six people you could use as references. Write their names, spelling them correctly. Then write their addresses and phone numbers. Remember, you shouldn't use relatives as references.

Lesson 2 Application Vocabulary

As Yolanda looked over her brother's application, she realized that there were some words on it that he might not understand. To help him, she gave him this list of words and their definitions. Understanding the meanings of these words will help you, as well, to do a better job filling out a job application.

Application Glossary

address   The place where you live, where your references can be reached, or where your school or employer is located. An address should include the number and street name, the city and state, and the ZIP code. Remember that a comma goes between the city and state, but no comma is used between the state and the ZIP code.

college   The name of the college or university you attended. You do not have to have graduated to include it.

company   The place where you work or the places where you have worked before.

course   The subject in which you majored in school. For example, in high school you might have taken an academic, a college preparatory, a business, an auto mechanics, or a general course.

degree   An award given if you graduated from a two-year or four-year college. For example, you might have earned an Associate of Arts, Bachelor of Arts, or Bachelor of Science. These degrees are usually written as A.A., B.A., and B.S.

experience   A term referring to other jobs that you have held. This section of the application may also ask for the dates worked at these jobs, the name of the companies, the addresses of the companies, your duties and titles, the names of your direct supervisors, and the reasons why you left these jobs.

position   Job or job title, such as short-order cook or receptionist.

references   The names, positions, addresses, and sometimes the telephone numbers of people who know you and can talk about the kind of person you are. They might tell how well you do things and how well you get along with others. References can include previous employers, friends, teachers, and clergy. Previous employers can only discuss job-related information when giving a reference.

signature   A handwritten (rather than typed or printed) name. Most applications require that you write, not print, your name somewhere near the bottom of the application.

Activity A Number your paper 1 to 10. Then write the correct answer from the box that completes each statement. (Use each answer only once.)

references	position	signature
course	address	college
companies	degree	experience
job application		

1) You will find a fact sheet helpful when you are filling out a _____.

2) Wherever you are asked to give an _____, you should write the complete information including the ZIP code.

3) An application may ask what _____ you took in high school.

4) The application may also ask if you went to _____ .

5) If you graduated from college, you may have to add what _____ you received when you graduated.

6) Any work you did at jobs before the one you are applying for is called _____ .

7) You may have to give the names of the _____ for whom you worked.

8) You may also have to say what _____ you are applying for.

9) You will probably have to give names, addresses, and telephone numbers of people who know you. These names are called _____ .

10) Near the end of the application, you will have to write your _____.

Activity B Number your paper 1 to 10. Then match each term in the first column with its definition in the second column.

Word

1) signature

2) address

3) company

4) references

5) college

6) course

7) position

8) degree

9) experience

10) job application

Explanation

a) the number of the house or building and the name of the street, city, state, and ZIP code

b) the name of the two-year or four-year college you went to

c) the name of the place where you worked

d) the subject in which you majored in school

e) what you get when you graduate from college

f) other jobs you have held

g) a form used in making a request to be hired

h) names of people who can say what kind of person you are and what kind of work you do

i) your written name

j) job

Place of birth

City and state or country where a person was born.

"Some phrases on applications," Yolanda explained to her brother, "can be a little confusing. For example, many applications ask for your **place of birth**. That doesn't mean the name of the hospital where you were born. It means the city and state where you were born." She added, "People who were born in another country should write the name of that country."

Yolanda handed Carlos a sheet of paper. "Here are other possibly confusing phrases you probably will find on most applications," she said. "It's a good idea to keep this list with your fact sheet so that you have it handy whenever your fill out an application."

Confusing Application Phrases

"Position applied for"
　The job or jobs you want

"List last or present employer first"
　Your employment record, starting with the last job you had or the job you currently have. Then list the job before that, and the job before that, and so on, until you have listed your very first job last. That section of an application might look something like this:

2001 to present:	Miller Supply Company
	1100 Grant Street
	Boston, MA 02109
1998 to 2001:	Homing Graphics
	1567 Sober Avenue
	Boston, MA 02110
1996 to 1998:	Grass Roots Garage
	100 Main Street
	Sturbridge, MA 01566

"Reason for leaving"
　The reason you left a job. Your reason might be that you learned new skills or changed careers, that the company went out of business, or that you were laid off.

"May we call your present employer?"
　A request to use your present employer for a reference. If you do not want to have your current supervisor know that you are looking for another job, answer No after this question.

"References"
　The names and addresses of people who can recommend you for a job. Give as many references as the application calls for. For example, if the application has three spaces for references, give three references.

Activity A Number your paper 1 to 5. Then match each item with the section of the application in which it belongs. Also, write the correct name of each item.

1) I want to get into a new line of work.

2) Mary Smith, typing teacher
Durant High School
8763 Clyde Boulevard
Salt Lake City, UT 84154
(801) 555-7463

Rev. James Deems, pastor
Thames Avenue Church
11 Thames Avenue
Salt Lake City, UT 84111
(801) 555-1146

3) waiter

4) yes

5) 2001 to present:

Fisher's Eatery
665 Laird Street
Salt Lake City, UT 84123

1999 to 2001:

Hank's Pizza Palace
2749 Flame Road
Salt Lake City, UT 84101

Using Yolanda's tips, Carlos completely filled out his job application. The company even called him back for another interview.

As Carlos continued to apply for jobs, he found that he still didn't understand all of the phrases on a few applications. As he came across various words or phrases, he wrote them down. Then one day he took his list to his sister. Yolanda used his list to make the guide sheet shown below.

Application Guide

"Kind of work desired"
  Means "What kind of job would you like to have?"

"Have you ever been employed by this company?"
  Means "Did you ever work before for this company?"

"Have you ever been employed by a similar concern?"
  Means "Did you ever work for a company that makes the same kind of product or offers the same kind of service as this company?"

"Is all the information on this application true? If we discover that it is not, that will be considered sufficient cause for dismissal"
  Means "If our company hires you and then finds out you did not tell the truth on your application, you could be fired."

"In case of emergency, notify"
  Means "If you have an accident or get sick, whom should the company call?"

"Final rate of pay"
  Means "before you left that job, how much were you being paid?" (refers to a previous job)

"Nature of work done"
  Means "What kind of work did you do on this job?" (refers to a previous job)

After Carlos looked over the application guide, Yolanda said to him, "There is no way you can be prepared for every question you will find on every application. Therefore, if you don't understand something, ask the person who gave you the application. Actually, asking questions can make a good impression because it tells the person that you really care about doing a good job on the application."

Activity A   Number your paper 1 to 7. Then write the word or phrase from the "Possible Answers" box that answers each question. (Use each answer only once.)

Possible Answers		
Mary Smith, mother	$6.00 per hour	No
Administrative Assistant	Yes, Smith & Sons	Yes
Filed and ran errands		

1) Kind of work desired?

2) Have you ever been employed by this company?

3) Nature of work done?

4) In case of emergency, whom should we notify?

5) Is all the information on this application true?

6) Have you ever been employed by a similar concern?

7) Final rate of pay?

Activity B   Suppose you were fired from your last job because you did not come to work regularly. What would you say on an application for a new job about your reason for leaving your last job? Would you tell the truth? Suppose there were good reasons why you did not go to work regularly. Write a short paragraph explaining what you would say on the application.

When you begin to fill out an application, there are seven important things you should remember. When you finish, check your application to make sure that you have done all of them correctly.

Take your fact sheet and the application checklist with you to make sure you fill out the application completely and accurately.

1. Follow all directions. If you are asked to type your application, type it. Otherwise, always use a pen.

2. If you are asked to print, print the information. Use capital letters where appropriate and lowercase letters otherwise—such as this example.

Medina	Carlos	J.
(PRINT) Last name	First name	Middle Initial

3. Make sure you fill in all blanks. If something does not apply to you, put **N/A** (for Not Applicable) on the blank line.

N/A

Not applicable; a term used on job applications when a section does not apply to the person applying for a job.

4. Make sure your application is neat and easy to read. If you have to make any corrections, be as neat as possible. For example, you could use an erasable pen or correction fluid, or you could ask to start over.

5. Make sure all the information that you give is correct. Use your fact sheet whenever necessary. Check to make sure that you have the correct spelling of the names of people, streets, cities, and states. Make sure that the street numbers, ZIP codes, and telephone numbers are also correct.

6. Be honest about all the information that you put on an application.

7. If possible, get someone else to check your application after you have checked it.

Activity A   Number your paper 1 to 10. If the statement is true, write *True* next to the number. If it is not true, write *False*.

1) A job application should be as perfect as you can make it.

2) If an application says that it should be typed, you could fill it out with a pen.

3) If something on an application does not apply to you, leave that section blank.

4) Some employers think that people who turn in messy applications will be undependable workers.

5) Give your fact sheet to a potential employer.

6) You should use the same fact sheet for years.

7) Use capital letters only where appropriate.

8) Always fill in an application with a pencil.

9) Check the spelling of all words on your application.

10) Never ask someone else to check your application for you.

A completed application says something about the kind of person you are. The better the application looks and the more accurate it is, the more likely you are to get the job. You must be honest about the information you give on an application because some companies will fire you if they find out that what you wrote on your application is not true.

You should prepare a fact sheet to help you fill out your application. Make sure the fact sheet is correct, and also make sure that you carefully copy the information from it.

Follow the directions on the application exactly, and provide as much information as you possibly can. When part of an application does not apply to you, write *N/A* in that section. This tells the person reading the application that you have left nothing out.

Make your application as neat as you possibly can. If you make a mistake, erase carefully, use correction fluid, or ask to start over. Remember that a job application tells people a great deal about you, and you want to make the best possible impression.

Part A   Number your paper 1 to 10. Then write short answers to these questions.

1) What are two reasons for preparing a fact sheet before you apply for a job?

2) What three kinds of information should you include in your fact sheet?

3) Why should you include information that you know by heart on a fact sheet?

4) If you are not sure how to spell a person's name, what should you do?

5) If you are not sure how to spell a street name or the name of a company, what should you do?

6) Why is it important to update your fact sheet every time you apply for a new job?

7) What seven things should you check when filling out an application?

8) Why is it important to turn in a perfect application?

9) If your application is incomplete or messy, what conclusion might an employer draw about you?

10) When is it acceptable to erase on an application?

Part B   Number your paper 1 to 10. Then write the correct answer from the box that completes each statement.
(Use each answer only once.)

directions	type	neat	capital
looks good	pen	N/A	lowercase
blanks	correct	Not Applicable	

1) You should follow all _____ on an application.

2) If an application tells you to _____ , you should type.

3) Use a _____ when you fill out an application.

4) When you print, you should use _____ letters where appropriate.

5) Use _____ letters everywhere else.

6) Make sure you fill in all _____ .

7) If something does not apply to you, put _____ , or _____ , on the blank line.

8) Make sure your application _____ and is easy to read.

9) If you must erase, be as _____ as possible.

10) All of the information on your application should be _____ .

Part C   Number your paper 1 to 10. Then write the information you would supply for each of these items that could appear on a job application. (Some items may not apply to you if you have never worked before. What should you write if something doesn't apply to you?)

1) Place of birth

2) Job applied for or position applied for

3) List last or present employer first

4) Final rate of pay

5) Nature of work done

6) Reason for leaving

7) May we call your present employer?

8) Kind of work desired

9) Have you ever been employed by this company?

10) In case of emergency, notify . . .

| Test Taking Tip | If you don't know the answer to a question, put a check beside it and go on. Then when you are finished, go back to any checked questions and try to answer them. |

5

Applying by Phone

Help-wanted ads in the newspaper often give telephone numbers for you to call. When you call these numbers, you need to know what to say and how to say it. How well you do will often determine whether or not you get invited to a company for an interview.

In Chapter 5, you will learn how to prepare for a telephone call to ask about a job and what to say during the conversation.

Goals for Learning

▶ To know what information you need before applying for a job by phone

▶ To know how to begin a telephone conversation positively when applying by phone

▶ To learn what information to get and to give when applying by phone

▶ To know how to end a conversation properly when applying by phone

Personnel

The part of a company that deals with the employees; personnel might hire people and keep records about how well they do their jobs. Another name for this department is human resources.

The telephone rang in the **personnel** division of Hilbert Electronics, a large company with many employees. Cynthia Dawson picked up the phone and said, "Good morning. Personnel division, Hilbert Electronics. May I help you?"

"Yeah," said the voice at the other end. "I want a job."

Cynthia sighed to herself and thought, "Here we go again." Then she asked politely, "What job are you interested in?"

"This here job you got advertised," replied a woman's voice on the other end.

"Ma'am, we have 12 jobs advertised. Which one are you referring to?" Cynthia asked.

"The one for a stock clerk," the woman answered.

"Was that stock clerk position for the supply warehouse or for the docks?" Cynthia inquired.

"Well, I don't know. Wait while I find out where that newspaper went. Here we go. Guess I want the job in the supply warehouse," the woman answered.

"Then the person you need to speak to is Radia Horowitz," said Cynthia. "I will transfer your call."

"I want to write that name down. Let me go get a pencil," said the woman.

After about three minutes more, Cynthia hung up the phone. Then she turned to her friend Ming Lee and said, "I'm really tired of talking to people on the phone who don't have the slightest idea of how to make a call—especially a call applying for a job. Sometimes I wish I could just hang up on them, but that would be rude."

Ming Lee laughed. "I know just what you mean," she said. "Sometimes I think we could make a fortune if we wrote a handbook about how to apply for a job on the telephone."

"What a good idea!" exclaimed Cynthia. "Let's write a handbook. We could send it out to people who call us to apply for jobs but don't know what to do. They might not get a job here, but the handbook would help them so that they wouldn't sound so bad to the next place they called."

"The first thing I'd put in the handbook would be something about having the information applicants need before they make a call," said Ming Lee.

"Right," said Cynthia. "Let's start a list."

Ming Lee and Cynthia started to make a list of the information people should have handy before they call to apply for a job. Here is what their list looked like.

Needed Information

1. The exact description of the job that was advertised

2. Where and when the job was advertised, including the name and date of the newspaper or job announcement

3. A fact sheet of information about education and work

4. Days and times when available for a job interview

5. Telephone number where applicant can be reached if a call back is necessary

Helpful Hints

1. Have paper and pencil available to write any information given during the call—such as the date, time, and place for an interview.

2. Cut out the ad from the newspaper and have it available when the call is placed.

It was clear to Cynthia and Ming Lee that applicants have to do some work before they ever dial a telephone number to apply for a job. If you want to make a **good impression** during a telephone call, you will also have to have all the information you need handy. If you are well prepared, the person you speak to probably will be impressed and will assume that you will be well organized on the job. This is just one way to make your first contact with a future employer a positive one.

Activity A   Number your paper 1 to 6. Then write short answers to these questions.

1) Why is it necessary to tell the exact job for which you are applying?

2) How will a fact sheet help you during a phone call to apply for a job?

3) Why should you tell where and when you saw the job advertised?

4) If you are asked when you can come in for an interview, why is it important that you answer immediately and accurately?

5) Why should you give a telephone number where you can be reached?

6) Why does having all the information you need make a good impression?

Activity B   On a sheet of paper, list the information you would need before you make a call to apply for the following job that was advertised in the *Pittsfield Chronicle* on November 23. (Be sure to refer to Ming Lee and Cynthia's list.)

> **STOCK CLERK** to work in supply warehouse. No exp. nec. Should be good in math. Needs computer exp. Call Mr. Neal at 555-0800.

"What do you think ought to come next?" Cynthia asked Ming Lee.

"Well, one of the things I hear from the people here in the personnel division is that callers don't identify themselves. It's also annoying when it takes some people a long time to get around to saying why they are calling," answered Ming Lee.

"You're absolutely right," Cynthia agreed. "Those are two complaints I've also heard."

Cynthia and Ming Lee decided that they would come up with some easy-to-understand rules about making phone calls in answer to job ads. After some thought, they decided on these three rules.

Rule 1   In a clear, distinct voice, give your first and last name.

Rule 2   Then say why you are calling. For example, you could say, "I'm calling in answer to your ad for a stock clerk that appeared in Sunday's *Pittsfield Chronicle*."

Operator

A person who connects and transfers telephone calls.

Rule 3   If an **operator** asks you to hold or says that you will be transferred to another person, wait. Then when the second person answers, repeat Rules 1 and 2.

Activity A   With a classmate or friend, practice beginning a telephone call in response to the ad to the left. (Refer to the three rules that Cynthia and Ming Lee wrote.)

STOCK CLERK
wanted for dock warehouse.
No exp. nec.
Call Mr. O'Leary,
555-7463.

When you practice, use these three different situations.

1) Mr. O'Leary is the person who answers the phone.

2) Mr. O'Leary's secretary answers the phone.

3) After an operator answers the phone, he transfers you to the personnel division. Someone there finally transfers you to Mr. O'Leary's secretary.

Activity B   Call a friend or relative. Ask that person to tell you if your voice is clear and easy to understand. Take notes on any comments or suggestions that he or she gives you.

Interviewer

The person doing the interview.

Cynthia and Ming Lee realized that once a person begins a telephone interview, it is hard to know what the **interviewer** will ask. However, they did think that some general guidelines might be helpful. For example, the first thing an applicant should remember is to try to make a good impression. To do that, the applicant must remember certain things about language and behavior.

Activity A   On a piece of paper, make three columns. Label them *Good, Bad,* and *Can Be Improved.* Then under each column, write what is good about this conversation, what is bad, and what could be improved.

Caller:	Hello, this is Joseph Fritz. I'd like to speak to Mr. O'Leary.
Operator:	One moment please. I'll connect you.
Secretary:	Hello, this is Marcia Hunt, John O'Leary's secretary.
Caller:	I want to speak to Mr. O'Leary.
Secretary:	May I ask in reference to what?
Caller:	Yeah, I'm calling about a job. What else?
Secretary:	What job is that, sir?
Caller:	Stock clerk.
Secretary:	Is that the stock clerk at the supply warehouse or the dock warehouse?
Caller:	(a little annoyed) The dock warehouse—if it makes any difference.
Secretary:	What are your qualifications for this job?

Caller:	I don't know. I never had a job like that before.
Secretary:	(sounding bored) Did you graduate from high school?
Caller:	Yeah, but can I talk to Mr. O'Leary now?
Secretary:	(coldly) Unfortunately, Mr. O'Leary is not available right now, but if you give me your phone number, I'll have him call you if he wants any more information.
Caller:	555-4952.
Secretary:	Thank you. (hangs up)

The Wrong Way

After Mr. O'Leary reads the summary of the conversation between his secretary and Joseph Fritz, do you think he'll call Joe back? Unfortunately, Joe probably lost the chance to get the job because of the mistakes he made.

- Joe didn't repeat his name to Mr. O'Leary's secretary or use the word *please*.
- He didn't state his purpose for calling without being asked.
- He didn't mention where he had seen the ad for the stock clerk's job.
- He didn't mention any qualifications he might have for the job.
- He didn't answer the secretary's questions politely. He was even rude.
- Overall, Joe gave the impression that he really didn't care about the job.
- Moreover, because Joe did not give all the information he should have given to Mr. O'Leary's secretary, he did not make a good impression on her.

What should Joe have said and done during this telephone conversation? What might have helped him make a good impression?

These are the steps Joe should have followed during his phone conversation.

1. He should have patiently and politely repeated his name and reason for calling to each person he spoke to.

2. He should have answered the question about qualifications by listing **personal qualifications** or characteristics that would have shown that he would have done a good job. For example, he could have said, "I had a good attendance record at school. I enjoy working with numbers, and I know how to keep very accurate records. If I am given directions, I follow them well."

3. He should not have used **slang**—such as *yeah*. He should have used correct English.

4. He should have used the last name of the person to whom he was speaking. Calling a person by name (when you know it) is polite and makes a good impression.

5. He should have asked for information he might need about the job. For example, he could have asked about the location of the job, the hours, and the type of work. (Some people prefer to discuss salary in person rather than over the phone.)

6. Finally, he should have found out if he could have an interview; if so, he should have asked for a specific time and place.

> *Personal qualifications*
>
> Traits that help one meet job requirements.

> *Slang*
>
> Language that is coarse, nonstandard, incorrect, or informal; for example, ain't or yeah.

Ming Lee is often the first person job applicants talk to when they call Hilbert Electronics. You should make a good impression on everyone you talk to when applying by phone.

Joe didn't reach Steps 5 and 6 because Mr. O'Leary's secretary cut him off. She had lost interest in talking with him and probably had decided that Joe was not the kind of person the company wanted to hire.

A Better Conversation

Here's what the conversation with Mr. O'Leary's secretary might have been like if Joe had handled it better.

Secretary:	Hello, this is Marcia Hunt, John O'Leary's secretary.
Joe:	Hello, Ms. Hunt. My name is Joseph Fritz. I'm calling in answer to your ad in Sunday's *Pittsfield Chronicle* for a stock clerk in your dock warehouse.
Secretary:	Just one minute; I'll put you through to Mr. O'Leary.
Mr. O'Leary:	This is John O'Leary.
Joe:	Mr. O'Leary, my name is Joseph Fritz. I'm calling in answer to your ad in Sunday's *Pittsfield Chronicle* for a stock clerk in your dock warehouse.
Mr. O'Leary:	Fine, Mr. Fritz. What are your qualifications for the job?
Joe:	Well, sir, I'm good at keeping accurate records. In fact, I kept records of the stock in a grocery store last summer. I also got good grades in math in school, and I had a good attendance record.
Mr. O'Leary:	Did you graduate from high school?
Joe:	Yes, Mr. O'Leary. I graduated in June. Can you tell me something about the job, sir? What would I be doing?

Mr. O'Leary:	You would be keeping the records of all incoming stock that is received at our dock warehouse. You would also be responsible for letting the foreman know when more stock has to be ordered.
Joe:	I know I could handle that, sir. Where would I be working?
Mr. O'Leary:	The warehouse is located at 110 Water Street.
Joe:	Yes, I know where that is.
Mr. O'Leary:	You sound like someone we'd like to hire, Joe. Can you come for an interview with me tomorrow at 10:00 A.M.?
Joe:	Yes, sir. Where should I come for the interview?
Mr. O'Leary:	My office is in the Steel Building on the corner of Maple and Evergreen Streets—Suite 553.
Joe:	(reading his notes) That's the Steel Building, Maple and Evergreen Streets, Suite 553, at 10 o'clock tomorrow morning.
Mr. O'Leary:	That's correct.
Joe:	Thank you, Mr. O'Leary. I'll be there. Good-bye.

Notice that Joe made a good impression on Marcia Hunt because he was prepared. This could be why she put him through to Mr. O'Leary.

Activity A Number your paper 1 to 8. If the statement is true, write *True* next to the number. If the statement is not true, write *False*.

Tone

The inflection or pitch of words used to express meaning, mood, or feeling.

1) Always keep your **tone** of voice polite and patient.

2) Give your name and the reason for calling to the first person who answers the phone. After that, just give your name.

3) If you don't have any work experience for the job advertised, list the personal qualifications that you think would help you to do a good job.

4) Use the name of the person to whom you are speaking.

5) Never use slang. Use correct English.

6) Take down all the information given and read it back to make sure that it is correct.

7) If you know the name of the person, you may use it when you are speaking.

8) Never ask questions about the job during an interview on the phone. Wait to ask questions about the job until you can speak to the interviewer in person.

Mr. O'Leary takes notes as he talks to Joe on the phone. The impression you make on the phone can help you get the job you want.

In addition to making certain he had written all the information correctly, Joe thanked Mr. O'Leary before saying good-bye. Cynthia and Ming Lee think that the way you end a conversation is almost as important as the way you begin it because people often remember the last thing they heard more than anything else.

Also remember that you should never make a conversation any longer than it has to be. Don't risk making the person you're talking to grow impatient and annoyed. Instead, save questions about details for the job interview.

Activity A   Number your paper 1 to 7. If the statement will help make a good impression, write *Good* next to the number. If the statement will help make a bad impression, write *Bad*. (Be prepared to explain why each statement is labeled *Good* or *Bad*.)

1) "Okay. Yeah, I'll come."

2) "Yes, sir. I'll be there."

3) "Don't talk so fast. I can't get all this stuff down."

4) "Last summer I didn't have a job, but now I think I should have. The experience would have been good. Actually, my mother wanted me to get a job."

5) "Gee, this is great! Of course, I'll come in for an interview. See you then."

6) "Would you mind going a little slower? I want to make sure that I get all this information down correctly."

7) "Thank you very much. I'll see you tomorrow morning at 10:00 A.M. in your office."

Chapter Summary

When you have to apply by telephone for a job, you need to make a good impression if you want to be invited for an interview. These suggestions should help you create that good impression.

1. Have the following information in front of you before you make a call:

    - the exact description or title of the job
    - how you found out about the job
    - your fact sheet
    - days and times when you are available for an interview
    - a telephone number where you can be reached

2. In a clear, distinct voice, give your name and the reason for your call.

3. Repeat your name and the reason for your call to each person you speak to.

4. Always be patient and polite.

5. Answer the questions you are asked as completely as necessary.

6. Avoid slang. Use good business English.

7. When you know the last name of the person to whom you are talking, use it.

8. Ask appropriate questions. Write down information you will need.

9. Thank the person before hanging up.

10. Do not make the conversation too long.

Part A   Number your paper 1 to 10. Then rewrite these activities in the order in which you would probably do them when applying for a job by telephone.

- Give the qualifications I have for the job.
- State which job I am applying for.
- Give my personal qualifications.
- Have my fact sheet and a pencil and paper handy.
- Give my name.
- Give the reason for my call.
- List the days and times I am available for an interview.
- Thank the person for his or her assistance and time.
- Repeat my name and the reason for my call if an operator answers.
- State where the job was advertised.

Part B   Number your paper 1 to 5. Then write short answers for these questions.

1) Why should you give your name and the reason for your call?

2) What should you do if you are asked to give your qualifications and you haven't had any work experience?

3) Why should you avoid using slang or incorrect English?

4) Why should you use the last name of the person to whom you are speaking?

5) Why is it helpful to read back the information that you have taken down?

Part C   Number your paper 1 to 15. If the statement is true, write *True* next to the number. If the statement is not true, write *False*.

1) Making a good impression is important when you call about a job.

2) It is not important to be polite to the operator who first answers the telephone.

3) Before you dial the phone, have all important information in front of you—such as what the job is, where it was advertised, and how you found out about it.

4) You only have to give your name to the operator.

5) When you are talking to a person about a job, your saying that you have no qualifications is being honest.

6) Even if you have never done a job before like the one advertised, you should mention related things that you do well.

7) You cannot talk too much during a telephone call because the more you say about yourself, the more the employer will like you.

8) It is a good idea to have pencil and paper handy.

9) If an employer asks you to come for an interview, make sure that you can be there on the day and time set.

10) If you make an appointment for an interview as soon as possible, an employer will think you are eager to get the job.

11) Give a telephone number where you can be reached.

12) Answer all questions politely and patiently.

13) Sounding enthusiastic and eager will probably help you get the job.

14) If you are more comfortable using slang, use it.

15) Even if you know the last name of the person to whom you are talking, it is not a good idea to use it.

Test Taking Tip If you don't understand the directions to a section of a test, read over the questions to see if you can figure out what you are supposed to do. If you still can't figure it out, ask the person giving the test, if possible.

Chapter

6

Being Interviewed

If you get an interview at a company, you have a good chance of getting a job there. That's why it's so important that you make a good impression at the interview. Of course, making a good impression begins long before the interview actually takes place and continues to the moment you walk out of the door after the interview is over.

In Chapter 6, you will learn what to do before an interview, what to do during an interview, and what to do at the end of an interview.

Goals for Learning

▶ To understand appropriate dress for an interview

▶ To understand the importance that neatness and cleanliness play in creating a good impression during an interview

▶ To be able to answer questions correctly and completely during an interview

▶ To know how to communicate successfully during an interview

Barry Cohen was very nervous the day before his job interview. His teachers, his parents, and his friends had all warned him that how he acted and looked would have a lot to do with whether or not he would get the job.

Barry really wanted this job because it was the kind of work he liked. The pay was good, and the company had good benefits. There was no doubt in his mind that the company would be a good place to work.

It made sense to Barry to do everything he could to make a good impression. As he thought about the interview, he decided that he should concentrate on three areas: how he looked and dressed, how good his answers to the interview questions were, and how well he communicated.

Barry's mother had told him, "When you are applying for most jobs, you should wear business clothes: a suit jacket and a tie." Then she had reminded him that everything he planned to wear should be clean and free of stains. As a result, Barry had taken his suit to the cleaners, and he had made sure that he had a clean shirt and tie. He had even polished his shoes.

Barry polishes his shoes the night before his job interview.

Then on the morning of the interview, he got up early enough to wash his hair, shower, and shave. Here are some other helpful hints for preparing for an interview.

Helpful Hints for Preparing for an Interview

- Make sure your hair is trimmed and combed neatly.

- Trim and clean your fingernails, use deodorant, and brush your teeth.

- Don't wear too much jewelry. Many chains or long, dangling earrings are not very businesslike.

- Wear clothes that make you look as if you are serious about working. A suit is a good choice. A skirt or pants with a shirt and jacket or sweater is also a good selection.

- Avoid loud colors that will distract from you. You want people to be tuned in to you, not to what you are wearing.

- Be as neat as possible. Make sure your clothes are pressed.

- Check the clothes you plan to wear to see if you need to make any repairs, such as replacing buttons or mending tears.

- When you are dressed and ready to go to the interview, check the way you look in a mirror. You could even ask someone else to check you over.

Because the people who interview you will judge you by your appearance first, you need to look good when you walk in. Just remember that looking good for a job interview is not the same as looking good for a dance or some other social event.

Activity A   On your paper, draw the following chart and label the three columns. Then write each of these items in the correct column.

brush teeth

get suit cleaned

iron shirt or blouse

replace buttons

shower

shave

wash hair

get a haircut

press clothes

use deodorant

shine shoes

clean and file nails

wear little jewelry

check yourself in a mirror

make needed repair

Preparing for an Interview		
Two or Three Days Ahead	**The Night Before**	**That Morning**

Activity B   Number your paper 1 to 6. Then write the correct answer from the box that completes each statement. (Use each answer only once.)

jewelry	suit
women	pants
bright and flashy	shirt
job	jacket
distract	businesslike
plain sweater	

1) When you go to a _____ interview, you should dress in a _____ manner.

2) A _____ is a good choice for both men and _____.

3) You could also wear a skirt or _____ with a _____ and _____ or a _____.

4) The colors of the clothes you wear should not _____ from you.

5) Do not wear _____ colors.

6) Be careful not to wear too much _____.

Receptionist

A person whose job it is to greet the public, answer questions, direct people to offices, etc.; the receptionist is often the first contact people have with a company.

Barry sat nervously in the waiting room. Finally, the **receptionist** said to him, "Ms. Mendez will see you now, Mr. Cohen." Barry made sure that he had thrown away his chewing gum because one of his teachers had said that chewing gum during an interview made a bad impression. Barry walked into Ms. Mendez's office tall and straight and then introduced himself.

"Hello, Ms. Mendez, I'm Barry Cohen. I'm here for an interview." He waited to sit down until Ms. Mendez offered him a chair. Then he sat patiently until she asked the first question.

During the interview, Barry listened carefully to each question. He thought about his answers and made sure he answered each question completely. He answered in a clear, easy-to-understand voice, and he looked at Ms. Mendez as he spoke. If he needed to be sure of a date or an address or the spelling of a name, he checked his fact sheet or résumé, which he had brought with him.

When the interview was over, Barry politely thanked Ms. Mendez for the interview and handed her a copy of his résumé. Then he asked her when he might hear from her.

Barry believed that he had handled the interview well. As an extra show of thanks, Barry sent Ms. Mendez a thank-you note.

Although there is no way you can guess all the questions you may be asked at an interview, remember that the aim of most questions is to determine if you are suited for the job. As a result, you should always answer truthfully and completely. If you don't know the answer to a question, say so politely.

Activity A Number your paper 1 to 5. Then list at least five things that Barry did that probably impressed Ms. Mendez.

Communication

The way or ways people let others know how they feel about something.

During an interview, **communication** is very important. There are several ways people communicate: their words, their attitude, and their body language. Body language usually includes how people sit or stand and how they look at others.

Alice Blue, the person Ms. Mendez interviewed after Barry, did not get the job because she did not communicate important information well. Alice had come into Ms. Mendez's office with her head down and had plopped into the chair nearest to the door. She mumbled the answers to the questions and sometimes used poor grammar and slang. When the interview was over, Alice left without saying anything. Alice did not get the job because she did not answer the questions carefully and her manners were poor.

On the other hand, Barry did get the job because he understood the importance of communication. He knew that how well he communicated could make the difference between getting a job and not getting it. He acted as if he really wanted the job.

Activity A   Number your paper 1 to 5. Write the letter of the best answer on your paper. Listed below and on page 104 are five situations that could happen during a job interview. Be prepared to explain why your choice is the best answer.

1) The interviewer asks you why you want the job. You say,

   a) "I need the money."

   b) "I'm interested in this kind of work and think that I can do a good job."

   c) "My father told me if I don't get a job, he's going to put me out on the street."

2) The interviewer asks you a question to which you do not know the answer. You say,

    a) "I read about that somewhere. It was in some magazine, I think."

    b) "Whatever you think."

    c) "I'm sorry. I don't know the answer to that question." Perhaps you could tell me what it is."

3) The interviewer tells you this job requires that you work one Saturday a month. You say,

    a) "I can manage that."

    b) "You've got to be kidding. I don't want to work on Saturdays."

    c) "I play baseball on Saturdays."

4) The interviewer asks you how your English grades were in school. You say,

    a) "I ain't never got nothin' lower than a *C*."

    b) "I is the best one in English in my family."

    c) "I got good grades in English."

5) The interviewer asks you why you were fired from your last job. You

    a) get angry and snap, "I don't know!"

    b) look down at the floor and mumble, "I don't know."

    c) look at the interviewer and say, "I don't know."

Chapter Summary

When you go for a job interview, you will make a good impression if you look and act your best. To look your best, you should wear businesslike clothes and be clean and neat. To look your best, you must also plan ahead in order to have things clean and in good repair on the day of the interview.

When you get to the interview, be polite. First, introduce yourself and tell why you are there. Then listen carefully so you answer the specific questions that you are asked. During the interview keep your attitude and body language positive. Also speak clearly, avoid slang, and use correct English. If you need help answering a question, you can look at your fact sheet. It's also a good idea to have a copy of your résumé with you. At the end of the interview, you should leave your résumé with the person who interviewed you.

Following these simple steps will help you get through a job interview without being too nervous. Remember, if you impress the person interviewing you, you will have a better chance of getting the job.

Part A   Number your paper 1 to 10. Then write the correct answer from the box that completes each statement. (Use each answer only once.)

cleaners	hair	time	bath	washing
shower	shave	ahead	deodorant	clean
nails	teeth	polish	communicate	

1) When you go for a job interview, everything about you should be _____ .

2) This statement means that you must plan _____ .

3) If you plan to wear clothing that cannot be washed, allow _____ to send the clothing to the _____ .

4) Make sure that things that need _____ are clean.

5) _____ your shoes.

6) Shampoo your _____, and men should also _____ .

7) Take a _____ or a _____ .

8) Be sure to use _____, and brush your _____ .

9) Clean and trim your _____ .

10) An interviewer knows that you care about getting the job when you _____ well.

Part B   Number your paper 1 to 10. If the statement is true, write *True* next to the number. If the statement is not true, write *False*.

1) Long, shaggy hair is fine for an interview if you are dressed neatly.

2) The interviewer will think that you lost a button just a few minutes ago if a button is missing from your shirt. A missing button will not mean that you look messy.

3) A collar that is not folded correctly may make you look messy.

4) If a seam is coming apart, fix it before you go to your interview.

5) When you need to repair something that you plan to wear to an interview, mend it neatly.

6) If you have a beard or a mustache, trim it.

7) Broken nails look okay.

8) Don't bother other people to find out how you look.

9) The color of your clothes is not important at all.

10) Always wear a suit to a job interview—regardless of what job you're applying for.

Part C On your paper, rewrite the information below. The new paragraph should show the *best* way to handle an interview.

> Bill slumped into the room and plopped down. He said, "Okay, what's the scoop?" When the interviewer asked a question Bill didn't know the answer to, Bill made something up. He forgot to bring his fact sheet, so he made up a date and an address. When he was told that the interview was over, he didn't say anything. He just got up and left.

Part D Number your paper 1 to 5. Then rewrite these sentences, correcting any errors.

1) Ain't I got an appointment?

2) My name be Patrick.

3) I doesn't know that.

4) Yeah, okay.

5) I think that you and me will get along fine.

Test Taking Tip If you do not know the meaning of a word in a question, read the question to yourself, leaving out the word. Then see if you can figure out the meaning of the word from its use in the sentence.

Chapter 7

Beginning a Job

Knowing what to expect when you start a new job will help you make a good impression on your new supervisors and fellow workers. The best advice to follow is to carefully read and follow all instructions and directions. If you have any questions, ask your supervisor because asking a few questions is better than making mistakes during your first weeks on a new job.

In Chapter 7, you will get some good advice that will help you get through the first weeks of a new job. You will also learn the areas that you will be evaluated on in your new job. If you know what they are, you can work hard at them from your first day on.

Goals for Learning

▶ To learn how to fill out a W-4 form

▶ To understand the importance of a company's rules and regulations

▶ To find places and things within a company

▶ To learn the main areas of a job evaluation

Allowances
Items that determine the amount of money to be withheld for a person's income tax.

Internal Revenue Service (IRS)
The government agency in charge of collecting taxes.

Personal allowances
Items you can claim on your W-4 form that reduce the amount of tax you have to pay.

W-4 form
An IRS form that decides the amount of money that will be taken out of your paycheck for income tax.

Withholding
An amount of money subtracted from your paycheck and given to the IRS as part or all of your income tax.

Although Shaun Owens and Bill Yee had never met before, they just happened to report to work at the same time for their first day at Beacon Industries. By the end of the first week, Shaun no longer had a job, but Bill was doing fine. What happened to them could also happen to you. For example, take a look at their first day.

The first thing that Shaun and Bill were asked to do was to fill out a form put out by the **Internal Revenue Service (IRS)** called a **W-4 form**. The law says that you must complete this form when you are hired so that your employer can hold back from each of your paychecks some of the taxes that you will probably owe the government at the end of the year. Shaun didn't know the first thing about the form, but Bill had filled out a W-4 before.

After having tried to fill out three forms, Shaun still didn't have one done correctly. On the fourth try, he made another mistake that would have caused more money to be taken out of his paycheck than was necessary. Bill, however, filled his form out correctly the first time because he had read and understood the instructions. Reading tax forms of any kind can be confusing, but some practice will help you understand them.

Understanding the following words on a W-4 form can also help to eliminate any confusion in your mind the next time you have to fill one out.

A **withholding** on a W-4 form is an amount of money that the company you work for subtracts from your salary. This part of your salary is paid directly to the IRS as part or all of your income tax.

Another word on W-4 forms is **allowances**. These are things the government will consider when deciding the amount of money that will be withheld from your salary as income tax.

You can claim from none to several **personal allowances**. For example, you can claim one personal allowance for yourself. Other personal allowances are described on the W-4 form. The more personal allowances you claim, the less money will be withheld

Deductions
Expenses considered when determining taxable income; you do not have to pay income taxes on such expenses.

Dependents
Children or other people who may not work and who count on you for over half of their needs.

Exemption
A reason why a certain amount of money does not have to be taken from your salary for income tax.

Spouse
Your husband or wife.

from your paycheck as taxes. Claiming fewer allowances, however, means that more money will be withheld. Of course, you must claim only the allowances that you are entitled to.

Dependents are a personal allowance. The W-4 form uses the word dependents to name children or other people who may not work and who count on you for over half of their needs such as food, shelter, and clothing.

You can claim another personal allowance for your husband or wife (your **spouse**). You can claim additional allowances if your spouse does not work.

On the W-4 form, an **exemption** is some reason why money does not have to be withheld as taxes from your pay. A **deduction** is an expense considered when determining taxable income; for example, you do not pay taxes on some expenses such as donations to charities, home mortgage interest payments, and state and local taxes.

Activity A Number your paper 1 to 7. Then match each income tax term in the first column with its meaning or explanation in the second column.

Term	Meaning
1) spouse	**a)** you can claim one for yourself
2) allowances	**b)** expenses the government considers when deciding what amount of money will be withheld from your paychecks
3) dependents	
4) deductions	**c)** expenses for which you do not have to pay taxes
5) withholding	
6) personal allowances	**d)** your husband or wife
	e) the part of your paychecks that is paid to the IRS as income tax
7) exemption	
	f) people who count on you for food, clothing, and shelter
	g) a reason why you don't have to have money withheld from your wages

Personal Allowances Worksheet

A   Enter "1" for **yourself** if no one else can claim you as a dependent . . . .   **A** _____

B   Enter "1" if:
- You are single and have only one job; or
- You are married, have only one job, and your spouse does not work; or
- Your wages from a second job or your spouse's wages (or the total of both) are $1,000 or less.   **B** _____

C   Enter "1" for your **spouse**. But, you may choose to enter -0- if you are married and have either a working spouse or more than one job (this may help you avoid having too little tax withheld). . . . .   **C** _____

D   Enter number of **dependents** (other than your spouse or yourself) you will claim on your tax return . . . .   **D** _____

E   Enter "1" if you will file as **head of household** on your tax return (see conditions under **Head of Household** above) . .   **E** _____

F   Enter "1" if you have at least $1,500 of **child or dependent care expenses** for which you plan to claim a credit . .   **F** _____

G   Add lines A through F and enter total here. **Note:** This amount may be different from the number of exemptions you claim on your return ▶   **G** _____

For accuracy, do all worksheets that apply.
- If you plan to **itemize or claim adjustments to income** and want to reduce your withholding, see the Deductions and Adjustments Worksheet on page 2.
- If you are **single** and have **more than one job** and your combined earnings from all jobs exceed $30,000 OR if you are **married** and have a **working spouse or more than one job,** and the combined earnings from all jobs exceed $50,000, see the Two-Earner/Two-Job Worksheet on page 2 if you want to avoid having too little tax withheld.
- If **neither** of the above situations applies, **stop here** and enter the number from line G on line 5 of Form W-4 below.

- - - - - - - - - - - - - - **Cut here and give the certificate to your employer. Keep the top portion for your records** - - - - - - - - - - - - - - -

Form **W-4**
Department of the Treasury
Internal Revenue Service

Employee's Withholding Allowance Certificate

▶ **For Privacy Act and Paperwork Reduction Act Notice, see reverse.**

OMB No. 1545-0010

1995

1 Type or print your first name and middle initial	Last Name	2 Your social security number

Home address (number and street or rural route)	3 ☐ Single ☐ Married ☐ Married, but withholding at higher Single rate.
	Note: *If married, but legally separated, or spouse is a nonresident alien, check the single box.*

City or town, state, and ZIP code	4 If your last name differs from that on your social security card, check here and call 1-800-772-1213 for a new card . . . . . ▶ ☐

5   Total number of allowances you are claiming (from line G above or from the worksheets on page 2 if they apply) .   **5** _____

6   Additional amount, if any, you want withheld from each paycheck . . . .   **6** $ _____

7   I claim exemption from withholding for 1995 and I certify that I meet **BOTH** of the following conditions for exemption:
- Last year I had a right to a refund of **ALL** Federal income tax withheld because I had **NO** tax liability.
- This year I expect a refund of **ALL** Federal income tax withheld because I expect to have **NO** tax liability.

If you meet both conditions, enter "EXEMPT" here . . . . ▶   **7** _____

Under penalties of perjury, I certify that I am entitled to the number of withholding allowances claimed on this certificate or entitled to claim exempt status.

Employee's signature ▶ _____   Date ▶ _____ , 19 ___

5 Employer's name and address (Employer: Complete 8 and 10 only if sending to the IRS)	9 Office code (optional)	10 Employer identification number

Activity A   On a separate sheet of paper, write the information you would fill out for items 1, 2, and 3 on the W-4 form shown on page 114.

1) Type or print your full name, home address (number and street or rural route), city or town, state, and ZIP code.

2) Your Social Security number

3) Marital status: Single
                     Married
                     Married, but withhold at higher single rate

Here's your chance to see if you could do as well as Bill did on his W-4 form. Read the following directions on the W-4 form. Then answer the questions in Activity B.

Activity B   Number your paper 1 to 6. Then write short answers for these questions about a W-4 form.

1) On line A, can you claim yourself if your parents claim you as a dependent? When can you claim yourself?

2) If you and your spouse both work, what can you enter on line C?

3) You are single and earned $1,987 on a second job. What do you enter on line B?

4) You have one job; your spouse doesn't work. Where do you enter the number *1*?

5) You have one job and are not married. Where do you enter the number *1*?

6) You have two children, ages three and five, who live with you. Your spouse works. What number do you enter on line D?

Your salary, the people who are your dependents, and your expenses will all determine how you complete a W-4 form. Because tax laws often change, you may need to have more or less money withheld from your paycheck from time to time. If you do not understand how to complete this form, ask your employer or someone in the personnel department of your company. You may also call the IRS to get help or to get the latest information.

Once Shaun and Bill had filled out their W-4 forms, they were given a list of the company's rules and regulations. They were told to read the list carefully because any employees who broke the rules could be fired.

Beacon Industries
Employees' Regulations

1. **Working Hours**

   Working hours are 8:30 A.M. to 5:00 P.M. You are allowed one 15-minute break daily. Your lunch period runs from 12:00 noon to 12:30 P.M. All employees are required to punch the time clock at the start and finish of each day and also before and after the lunch break. You are responsible for your own **time card**. It is forbidden for you to punch another person's time card. You will be paid according to the record shown on your time card.

2. **Employee Status**

   All new employees will be considered on **probation** for the first six months they are employed. Employees may also be placed on probation at any time if their work is less than satisfactory for any given evaluation period.

3. **Wage Policies**

   After six months of satisfactory service, you will receive a pay raise and be removed from probation status. Other pay raises will be given annually. You will be paid each Friday for the work done the week before.

Time card

A card used with a time clock to record each employee's starting and quitting times during each day on the job.

Probation

A period of time workers have to prove that they can do a job.

Activity A   Number your paper 1 to 10. If the statement is true, write *True* next to the number. If the statement is not true, write *False*.

1) At Beacon Industries, employees can eat whenever they want as long as they don't take over 30 minutes.

2) You must be at work by 8:30 A.M., and you may leave at 5:00 P.M.

3) You get one 15-minute break every day.

4) You must punch the time clock four times each day.

5) You can punch other peoples' time cards for them if they are in a hurry.

6) Your pay will depend upon what time your supervisor says you worked.

7) For the first six months that you work at Beacon Industries, you will be on probation.

8) If your work isn't good, you can be placed on probation at any time during your employment.

9) When you get off probation after working for the company for six months, you will get a raise.

10) You will get a pay raise once every six months.

11) If you do not follow the Employees' Regulations, you may be fired.

12) The Employees' Regulations provide information about the length of time in an evaluation period.

Activity B   If you begin work on Monday, March 5, when will you get your first paycheck? Remember, according to the company's rules and regulations, you will be paid each Friday for the work that you did the week before.

More Regulations

Shaun and Bill continued to read the company's rules. With discouragement in his voice, Shaun said, "There seems to be rules about everything. You can't do anything around here!"

"I think the rules make sense," Bill said. "Beacon has a business to run. You can't expect to be able to do just what you want to." He added, "These rules seem fair to me."

Workstation

The place where employees work or do a certain part of their job.

Sexual harassment

Doing or saying something sexual to someone who does not welcome it.

> ### General Rules and Regulations
>
> 1. You are expected to be at your **workstation** by 8:30 A.M. If you are sick, you must call your supervisor by 8:30 A.M. Absence and lateness on a consistent basis will be grounds for dismissal.
>
> 2. Smoking is not permitted inside the building for reasons of health and safety.
>
> 3. You should never use the telephone for personal business except for an emergency.
>
> 4. If your supervisor rates your work unsatisfactory, you will be given six months in which to bring up your rating. If you have not done so by that time, you will be dismissed.
>
> 5. Any employee proven to be guilty of **sexual harassment** is subject to automatic dismissal and possible criminal charges.

Activity C Number your paper 1 to 9. Then write short answers to these questions.

1) It takes you half an hour to get to work. You are due at your workstation at 8:30 A.M. You can get a bus that leaves your corner at 7:40 A.M., another that leaves your corner at 7:50 A.M., and another that leaves your corner at 8:00 A.M. Which bus or buses should you take to get to work? Why?

2) If you are going to be out sick, what should you do?

3) Why is smoking not permitted in the building?

4) If you get an emergency call during working hours, what will happen?

5) Why might it be a good idea to tell your family and friends not to call you at work unless there is a real emergency?

6) In June your supervisor rates your work as unsatisfactory. By what month must you bring up that rating? What will happen if you don't improve your rating?

7) How could someone at Beacon Industries get into trouble as a result of sexual harassment?

8) Is Shaun's attitude good or bad? Why?

9) Is Bill's attitude good or bad? Why?

Lesson **4**   **Finding Places and Things Within a Company**

After Shaun and Bill had read the company rules, they were sent to their workstations. Because Beacon Industries is in a large building, they were given a floor plan, or a map, to help them find their way. Shaun was to report to work area B, and Bill was to report to work area D.

Here is a copy of the floor plan they both received.

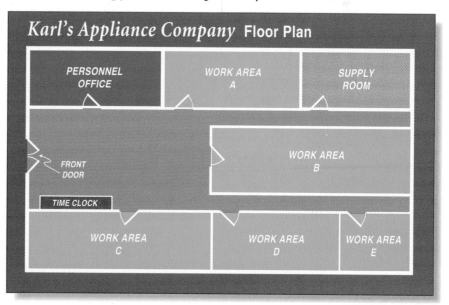

Karl's Appliance Company **Floor Plan**

| PERSONNEL OFFICE | WORK AREA A | SUPPLY ROOM |

FRONT DOOR

WORK AREA B

TIME CLOCK

| WORK AREA C | WORK AREA D | WORK AREA E |

Thinking that he didn't need to use the floor plan, Shaun walked out of the personnel office and went right into the supply room. Terribly embarrassed, he quickly pulled out the floor plan to find his way to his work area.

Activity A   Number your paper 1 to 10. Then write short answers to these questions about the floor plan of Beacon Industries.

1) Why do you think the time clock is placed near the front door?

2) If you had to go from work area C to work area E, in what direction would you turn when you walked out of the door of work area C?

3) Which work area is farthest away from the personnel office?

4) Once they have punched the time clock, which workers will get to their work area first?

5) Which work area is the largest?

6) Which work area is the smallest?

7) How many supply rooms are there?

8) Which work area does not share a wall with any office or work area?

9) Why do you think the personnel office is near the front door?

10) How many work areas are shown on this floor plan?

Activity B   On a separate sheet of paper, draw a floor plan of the first floor of your house or the apartment where you live. Then write five questions about that floor plan. Working with a classmate, trade floor plans and answer the questions.

As soon as Shaun and Bill got to their work areas, each of them was given a set of safety rules. Their supervisors told them to read the rules before they did anything else. Here are the rules they were given.

Beacon Industries

Safety Regulations

1. Do not operate any machine for which you have not been trained unless you are being supervised by an officially appointed employee.

2. Be sure all safety devices are in place before operating any machine.

3. In case of a breakdown or faulty operation, shut off all machinery and report to your supervisor.

4. Long hair, open-toed shoes, neckties, rings, loose clothing, and jewelry of any kind are forbidden in the work areas. Keep your clothes and valuables in the **locker** that was assigned to you.

These rules come under the U.S. Occupational Safety and Health Administration (OSHA).

Locker

A compartment where one can store personal belongings.

Shaun glanced at the rules before he began to walk around his workstation. Although he didn't know what a large switch was for, he pushed it anyway. Suddenly he heard a loud, shrill noise. Then his supervisor yelled out, "Turn off that machine! It's jamming!"

When the supervisor found out that Shaun had pushed the switch, he got angry. "Look," he shouted at Shaun, "the safety rules say that you aren't supposed to touch anything until someone is there to show you how to work the machine!" Once again Shaun was embarrassed.

Down in work area D, Bill spent a few minutes reading the safety rules before he told his supervisor that he was ready to learn how to use the machines in his area.

Activity A Number your paper 1 to 6. Then complete these safety rules for Beacon Industries.

1) You are not to try to work any machine unless _____.

2) All _____ before you operate any machine.

3) In case the machine breaks, _____ and _____.

4) If the machine is not working right, _____ and _____.

5) The following things are forbidden in the work areas: _____, _____, _____, _____, _____, and _____.

6) _____ are supplied as a safe place in which employees can keep clothing and valuables.

The Outcome

All week Shaun did just what he felt like doing. He got to work late, and one day he didn't go to work at all. To make matters worse, he didn't even call to say that he would be out that day. Worst of all, however, he did not learn how to use all of the machines properly. In fact, he caused one of the machines to break down. It took two days to get it repaired, and that delay cost the company a lot of money.

Bill, on the other hand, did just what he was told to do. He paid attention and learned fast. He followed all the rules, got to work a few minutes early every day, and was never absent. He was polite and helpful to the people around him. Even though he made a few mistakes, his supervisor didn't get angry because he knew that Bill was trying to do a good job.

At the end of the week, Shaun was fired. Bill was off to a good start at Beacon Industries.

Evaluation

Evaluation

A judgment about how well a worker does a job; many companies use a standard form to judge all employees on a regular basis.

Immediate supervisor

The person who has direct charge of you on the job; your boss.

Promotion

A raise in rank or position; it may include a pay raise.

Nearly all companies judge the performance of their employees on a regular basis. This type of **evaluation** is usually done by an employee's **immediate supervisor**. How well employees do on an evaluation can determine whether or not they keep their job, get a **promotion**, and/or get a pay raise.

If you are anything like Bill Yee, you will want to do well on each evaluation. It is helpful to know the areas in which you are evaluated. While evaluations vary from one business to another, most have some common areas that supervisors consider when judging performance. These six questions are often included on most evaluations.

Evaluation Criteria

1. **How well do you know your job?**

   If you do not need to be told over and over again what to do, you probably will be rated high on this item.

2. **What is the quality of your work?**

   If you make only few mistakes and finish each job, you will probably be rated high on this item.

3. **How much work do you produce?**

   If you work at a good pace and stay on schedule, you probably will score high on this item.

4. **How dependable are you?**

   If you follow directions and regulations, you probably will score high on this item.

5. **What kind of attitude do you have?**

   If you are cooperative, if you take pride in the job you do, and if you get along with your coworkers, you probably will score high on this item.

6. **What is your attendance like?**

   If you come to work regularly and are not late, you will probably score high on this item.

You will be a good employee if you learn to do your job well, work accurately, and turn out the amount of work expected of you. You also need to be dependable, have a positive attitude, and come to work regularly and on time. If you are this kind of an employee, you not only won't get fired like Shaun did, but you probably will get promotions and pay raises.

Activity B   Number your paper 1 to 9. Then after reading the following descriptions of nine workers, write the area in which each one seems to be weak. (Refer back to the six areas of evaluation on page 121.)

1) Mary has worked for the company for six months. She never seems to know what she should do. She always has to wait until her supervisor tells her what to do next.

2) B.J. works at a job where he is expected to turn out a certain number of items each day. Still, he thinks he needs to take several long breaks throughout the day.

3) Maya's carelessness often results in her supervisor having to redo or repair some of her work.

4) Nathan comes to work regularly, but he was late 14 times in the past 30 days. However, he always has some excuse—such as the bus was late or his alarm clock didn't go off.

5) Selma really gets annoyed when her supervisor points out something she is doing wrong. She sulks and then takes her anger out on the people around her.

6) Ella does what she wants to do when she wants to do it. She can be a good worker when she feels like it, but she often ignores the company's rules.

7) Raul is well liked by his supervisor and his coworkers. However, because he doesn't always pay attention to directions, he makes a lot of mistakes.

8) Rosa misses a lot of time from work because she always seems to have something wrong with her.

9) Isaac does a good job most of the time; however, he works for a company where the employees must work odd shifts and must work overtime at some busy times. He never offers to work an odd shift and never offers to work overtime.

During the first few days on a new job, you will have to fill out a W-4 form so that your employer knows how much money to withhold from each of your paychecks. This money goes to the Internal Revenue Service as payment of all or part of your income tax. It is important that this form be filled out correctly so that the proper amount of money is withheld. If too little money is withheld, you may have a large tax bill at the end of the year. If too much money is withheld, you may not take enough wages home to pay all your bills.

You will also need to read and understand the company's rules and regulations. If you do not understand them, ask your supervisor to explain them. If you don't follow them, you may lose your job. The government and most companies also have safety rules to keep their employees from getting hurt, to keep the machinery from getting broken, and to follow the rules of their own insurance policies. More and more companies are not allowing smoking on the premises, and some have strong penalties for sexual harassment on the job. You should respect these rules and live by them.

If you work for a large company, it's important that you know your way around. Some companies provide new employees with floor plans; others use signs posted around the building. If your company doesn't help you in either of these two ways, it's up to you to ask questions and to learn your way around the building.

Because the first few days on a job can be confusing and frustrating, give yourself some time to adjust and learn the rules and regulations. However, if you take your time, ask questions, and follow the rules, you should do well. Because most companies have some way to judge workers, doing well will help you to get promotions and pay raises.

Part A Number your paper 1 to 10. Then write the correct answer from the box that completes each sentence. (Use each answer only once.)

Social Security	W-4 form	spouse
personal allowance	salary	dependents
Internal Revenue Service	earn	withhold
exemption		

1) A _____ is filled out by everyone who works.

2) This form is used to decide how much your employer will _____ from your paycheck.

3) The money subtracted from your pay is paid to the _____ for part or all of your income tax.

4) On the form you may take a _____ for yourself.

5) If you are married and your _____ does not work, you may take an additional allowance.

6) On the form, children who count on you for over half of their needs are considered _____.

7) How much you _____ on the job will determine if you can claim an additional allowance.

8) A fixed amount of money you are paid for work done is your _____.

9) An _____ is a reason why you do not have to have money withheld from your wages.

10) You always have to write your _____ number on the form.

Part B Number your paper 1 to 15. If the statement is true, write *True* next to the number. If it is not true, write *False*.

1) Nearly all companies have some kind of employee evaluation.

2) The time clock is usually found farthest from where the employees enter the building.

3) If you need to be told over and over again how to do your job, you will probably be rated well for being curious.

4) If you want to be rated well on the quality of your work, you must be accurate and thorough.

5) If you don't produce as much work as your company thinks you should, you can get a low evaluation in that area.

6) Employees are never evaluated on whether or not they follow company rules and regulations.

7) Your attitude can affect your evaluation.

8) Attendance is important when you are evaluated, but whether or not you are often late doesn't matter.

9) The way you get along with the other employees may affect your evaluation.

10) Knowing your job is an important part of getting a good evaluation.

11) Your immediate supervisor is often the person who does the evaluation.

12) It is helpful to keep in mind the traits on which you will be evaluated.

13) On an evaluation, the quality of your work won't count as much as the quantity of the work you produce.

14) Knowing the company's rules and regulations won't make any difference on an evaluation.

15) A floor plan will help you find your workstation in a company.

Test Taking Tip When taking a true-false test, look for words such as *many, some, sometimes, usually,* and *may.* These words mean that the statement can have exceptions.

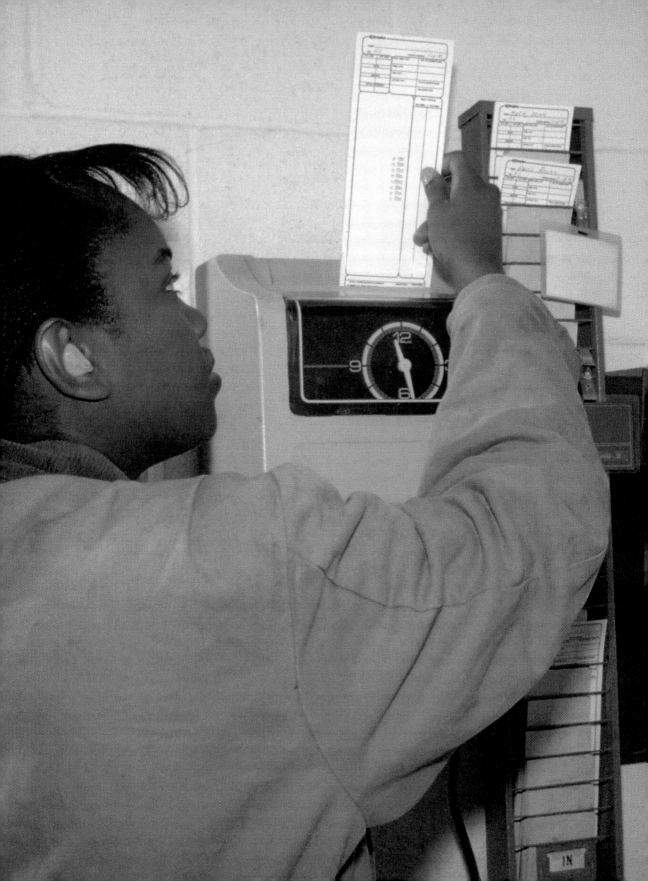

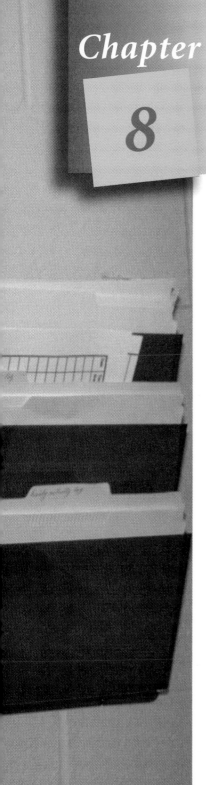

Learning How to Get Along

The first couple of weeks of a new job usually include learning many new tasks—everything from filling out time cards to running complicated machinery. If you know how to follow directions carefully, you should do very well.

In Chapter 8, you will learn that following directions is an important part of being successful in a new job. You will also discover some "tricks" like note taking that will help you remember important directions.

Goals for Learning

▶ To be able to fill in a weekly time card

▶ To know how to read a work schedule

▶ To understand the importance of reading and following both written and oral directions carefully

▶ To learn how to take notes to help you remember the details of important tasks

The first week on her first job was wonderful for Violet because her supervisor had assigned Tony Fusco to be her "buddy." His job was to help her through any new situations—such as filling out company paperwork and learning to use the sorting machine. Because of Tony's help, Violet did very well on her first day.

When she got to work on the second day, she realized that no one had shown her how to fill in a time card. Just then Tony came through the front door. "Hi, Violet," he said. "I'm glad I ran into you this morning because I forgot to show you how to fill out a time card yesterday."

As Violet filled out her time card, Tony watched and answered any questions she had. The time card had a heading that looked like this:

Date _____ / _____ / _____   _____ / _____ / _____
              From   To

WEEKLY TIME CARD

(Notice: This card must be turned in to the proper authority before payment can be made.)

Name _____

Address _____

Position _____ Dept. _____

Soc. Sec. No. _____ Badge No. _____

Pay week

One pay period of seven days.

The time card seemed pretty simple. Still, Violet wasn't sure what to put in the blank marked *Date*. Tony explained that at their company the **pay week** started on Monday. Since today was Tuesday, the first date Violet should put in was yesterday's date. That would take care of the *From* part of the blank. Then she was to put in the coming Friday's date. That would take care of the *To* part of the blank. Tony explained to Violet that she had to fill out a new time card every Monday.

Position

A job or job title; the name of the job that an employee does or the work for which one has been hired.

Violet also wanted to know what was meant by **Position**. Tony explained that that line was for the name of Violet's job. "Oh, that's easy!" she exclaimed. "I'm a sorting machine operator."

"Right," said Tony. "Any other questions?"

"No, I'm fine now," smiled Violet, "thanks to you."

Activity A   Number your paper 1 to 6 three times. Then, next to each number, write the letter of the item that each employee would put on that line of the following time card.

The Hall Distribution Company
EMPLOYEE TIME CARD

Date _____ / **(1)** / _____   _____ / **(2)** / _____
            From   To

Employee's Full Name _____ **(3)** _____

Position _____ **(4)** _____   Foreman _____ **(5)** _____

Signature _____ **(6)** _____

---

1) a) Bill Aziz

   b) 1/13/01

   c) Violet B. Deever

   d) *Violet B. Deever*

   e) 1/7/01

   f) sorter

2) a) *Frank D'Angelo*

   b) 1/20/01

   c) packer

   d) 1/14/01

   e) Frank D'Angelo

   f) Sonja Rosoff

3) a) shipping clerk

   b) 1/26/01

   c) 1/20/01

   d) Roger Martin

   e) *Roger Martin*

   f) Consulla Santos

Work schedule

A plan that shows the exact hours or shift each employee will work during a given pay period.

Shift

A scheduled period of work or duty; for example, a shift could be from 9:00 A.M. to 5:00 P.M. or from 7:00 P.M. to 3:00 A.M.

As they walked to their work area, Tony told Violet that each Monday she should check the **work schedule**. "This is not a nine to five place," he told her. "Our hours vary depending upon the workload. Some weeks you may have to come in early and leave early or come in late and leave late because we have an extra **shift** working."

That Friday, Violet went to the bulletin board in her work area and checked the work schedule. Tony had been right. Starting Monday, she was scheduled to work from 6:00 A.M. to 2:30 P.M.

On Monday, when Violet reported to work a few minutes before 6:00, her supervisor was pleased. He told her that some new people forget to check the work schedule. As a result, they lose pay because they don't get to work on time. (If Violet had reported to work at 8:00 A.M. instead of 6:00, she would have lost two hours of pay. If she were paid $7.75 an hour, how much would she have lost if she had been two hours late? If you figured $15.50, you were right.)

Here is the work schedule that Violet had checked on Friday.

WORK SCHEDULE—WEEK OF 1/14	
	Shift
Canos, Anika	3:30 P.M.
Carting, Ed	6:00 A.M.
Deever, Violet	6:00 A.M.
Fusco, Tony	8:30 A.M.
Glassman, Sylvia	8:30 A.M.
Moore, Simon	8:30 A.M.
Ratz, Bob	6:00 A.M.
Wu, Ai-Ling	8:30 A.M.

Notice that the line at the top tells what week this schedule is for. At the left are the employees' names. In the right-hand column are the times they are to report to work. There are three shifts, or scheduled work periods, at Violet's company.

Activity A   Number your paper 1 to 9. Then write short answers to these questions about the work schedule on page 130.

1) At what time do each of the three shifts report to work?

2) Do Violet and Tony work on the same shift this week?

3) Who works on the same shift with Tony?

4) Who works on the same shift with Violet?

5) Who works on the 3:30 P.M. shift?

6) What week does this schedule cover?

7) How many workers does this schedule include?

8) At what time does Simon Moore report to work?

9) At what time does Bob Ratz report to work?

Activity B   Figure out the time when each of the three shifts ends if each employee works an $8 \frac{1}{2}$ hour shift.

Activity C   The work schedule on page 130 was changed for January 16 because of a problem with the equipment. Fusco, Glassman, and Moore were to report four hours later than scheduled. Deever, Carting, and Ratz were to report three hours later than scheduled. Wu was to report two hours and thirty minutes earlier than scheduled. Canos was to report three hours and forty-five minutes earlier than scheduled. Rewrite the work schedule for January 16.

Violet had done very well following directions during her first week on the job. When she wasn't sure about something, she asked someone she could trust like Tony. She knew that reading and following directions would help her make as few mistakes as possible.

Because Violet's job required lifting and moving heavy boxes, she read the following rules. Her supervisor also told her that her **insurance coverage** may not pay benefits if she is injured as a result of not following such safety procedures.

Insurance coverage

Benefits included within the scope of an insurance policy or protective plan; the risks covered by the terms of an insurance contract.

Lifting and Moving Boxes

1. Check the area in which you will be moving the boxes.

2. Clear the floor of all objects that may cause you to trip.

3. Make sure the boxes will fit through doorways.

4. To lift, squat close to the box with one foot beside it and one foot behind it. Grasp the box in both palms and fingers. Keep both arms close to the body. Lift the box by straightening both legs.

5. To put the box down, reverse the lifting procedure. Let one side of the box touch down first so that hands are not trapped under the box. If your position has to be shifted, set the box down on a sturdy support.

WARNING: Employee's insurance coverage will not be effective if proper lifting procedures are not followed.

These directions are provided by the United States
Occupational Safety and Health Administration (OSHA).

Activity A Number your paper 1 to 5. Then put these directions for the correct way to lift and carry a box in the correct order by writing the letter next to the number.

a) Check to see if the doorways are wide enough for the boxes.

b) When putting the box down, let one side of the box touch first so that you can get your hands out.

c) Check the area in which you will be moving with the box.

d) Squat close to the box. Put one foot beside the box. Put the other foot behind it. Hold the box in both hands close to your body. Lift the box by straightening both legs.

e) Clear the floor and the surrounding area of anything that is in your way.

Activity B The warning at the end of the directions states, "Employee's insurance coverage will not be effective if proper lifting procedures are not followed."

1) Rewrite that statement in your own words. Make sure that you keep the real meaning of the statement.

2) Write the answers to these questions.

a) What could happen to Violet if she did not follow these directions for lifting and moving boxes?

b) Why would she lose her insurance coverage if she did not follow the lifting procedures?

Violet followed Tony's directions for lifting heavy boxes.

Written Directions

During the second week, Violet's supervisor gave her a small booklet and said, "These are directions for keeping your machine in the best possible running condition. Read them and make sure you follow them. If you have any questions, just ask me."

Violet read the directions carefully. Then she made herself a **schedule**. After you read the directions, decide why Violet made a schedule.

Schedule

A plan that shows the time and order of each job.

The Care of the Sorting Machine

1. Always turn the machine off when you leave the work area.

2. Oil the starter mechanism once each week.

3. Oil the rotary wheels once a day.

4. Oil the tray lifts once a month.

5. Dust the machine daily with an oiled cloth before using.

6. Do not try to repair the machine yourself. If something goes wrong, notify the supervisor immediately.

Violet made a schedule because there were some things she had to do every day, some things once a week, and some things once a month. Here's her schedule.

First (every day)—Dust with oiled cloth.

Second (every day)—Oil rotary wheels.

Monday—Oil starter.

First Monday of the month—Oil tray lifts.

Reminder 1: Turn OFF machine when you leave work area.

Reminder 2: If anything goes wrong, call supervisor.

Violet tacked her schedule onto her worktable and checked it off once she had done what she was supposed to do. She was smart not to trust her memory with so many important tasks.

Activity C   Number your paper 1 to 8. Then after you read the directions in the box, write short answers to the following questions.

Using the Copying Machine

1. Turn on "Start" button. When orange light under button stops blinking, insert paper.

2. Insert paper in tray marked with size of paper you are using.

3. Use no more than three inches of paper at a time.

4. Place copy face down on glass tray.

5. Close lid.

6. Push "Quantity" button until number of copies desired appears.

7. Push "Print" button.

8. Remove finished copies from tray at lower left side of machine.

---

1) How much paper can you use at one time?

2) What number should appear by the "Quantity" button?

3) Where do you put the paper?

4) How do you insert the copy?

5) Where will you find the finished copies?

6) When do you put the paper in?

7) How do you get the machine to start copying?

8) Can you use more than one size paper in this machine?

Activity D Number your paper 1 to 10. Read these directions for using a computer printer. Then write *True* or *False* for each of the following statements.

Guidelines for Using Media in Office Computer Printer

1. Put all media and envelopes print side down in the IN tray of the printer.

2. For plain paper, the print side has a symbol or word on the package to show that it is the print side.

3. For paper with a letterhead, load the letterhead side down and forward in the tray.

4. For transparencies, load the rough or uneven side down with the adhesive side forward in the tray.

5. For glossy paper, load the glossy side down.

6. Load only one type of media at a time.

7. When using index or postcards, make sure the right side of the card is aligned with the left side of the raised card guide.

8. Never use more than $\frac{1}{2}$ inch of media, $\frac{1}{4}$ inch of cards, or 20 envelopes at one time.

---

1) Put paper print side down in the IN tray of the printer.

2) For glossy paper, put the glossy side down.

3) You may load more than one kind of media at a time.

4) You cannot use postcards in this printer.

5) Plain paper has a symbol or word on the package to show the print side.

6) Never use more than $\frac{1}{2}$ inch of cards at one time.

7) When you use transparencies, put the rough side up.

8) When you use paper with a letterhead, put the letterhead side down and back.

9) Use no more than 20 envelopes at one time.

10) Index cards can be used in this printer.

Oral directions

Instructions given by word of mouth; spoken rather than written orders.

During her first few weeks on the new job, many people gave Violet **oral directions**. Violet quickly realized that she was having trouble remembering everything people were telling her. As a result, she got herself a small notebook and kept it—along with a pencil—in the pocket of her shirt. When someone began to tell her something, she would grab the notebook and take notes.

At first she would try and write every word that someone said. But this took too much time. Sometimes she would miss what someone was telling her because she was so busy writing. She learned that she didn't have to write every word people said— just the most important, or **key words**, to help her remember what they had said. She found that taking notes helped her and saved her from asking the same questions over and over again.

Key words

Important words that give the main idea; clues or aids used to help people remember information.

On Violet's second day, for example, Tony had told her, "When you start the sorter, set the dial on 5. Once it is working smoothly, move it slowly up to 7. Never put the dial past 7 unless the supervisor tells you to."

This is what Violet wrote in her notebook.

> Set 5, when working smoothly, move slowly to 7. Never past 7.

She included all the important ideas and left out those things she would remember once she saw what she had written. For example, when she saw "set 5," she knew she would know to set the sorter correctly when she started it.

Later that same day, her supervisor had told her, "The paper loader should never get below a thousand. Refill the loader at about 1500." Violet wrote this in her notebook.

> Refill paper loader—1500.

That was all she needed to write down because it was the most important information.

Activity A Have a partner read you the information in the box. Write down the key words or ideas from these oral directions on a piece of paper. The words should be what you would need in order to remember the directions.

"When the mail comes in, the first thing you want to do is sort it according to office. You'll find a list of the offices in the company directory that is on the counter right there. After the mail is sorted, you deliver the mail. The first mail you deliver is to Mr. Gaudet, the president. After that the order doesn't matter. Don't linger. All the mail should be delivered in twenty minutes. See this mail sheet? The secretary in each office must initial it when you deliver the mail. Bring that sheet back with you and put it in the file under 'Mail Sheets.' Put it in the front of the file right in front of the last one."

It is easy to see why Violet made a good start at her new job. She was careful to get paperwork done correctly. She asked questions when she had to learn what to do, and she read and followed written directions carefully. When people gave her oral directions, she took notes to help her remember later what had been said. You would do well to follow Violet's example when you start a new job.

Part A   Number your paper 1 to 5. Then write the information that an employee might fill in next to each number on this time card.

> ## The Hall Distribution Company
> ### EMPLOYEE TIME CARD
>
> **(1)**
> _____
> Employee's Name (print)
> **(2)**
> _____
> Position
> **(3)**
> _____
> For Week Beginning
> **(4)**
> _____
> Social Security Number
> **(5)**
> _____
> Employee's Signature

Part B   Number your paper 1 to 5. If the statement about the following work schedule is true, write *True* next to the number. If it is not true, write *False*.

WORK SCHEDULE	
Employee	**Starting time**
Anderson, Lee	7:30 A.M.
Chin, Weijen	8:00 A.M.
Green, Hazel	9:00 A.M.
O'Leary, Daniel	9:30 A.M.

This week each employee is asked to put in one hour of overtime each day.

1) The company staggers the time its employees arrive at work and leave work.

2) Lee Anderson gets to work two hours earlier than Hazel Green.

3) If the employees normally put in an $8\frac{1}{2}$ hour day, Weijen Chin would leave work at 4:30 P.M.

4) Lee Anderson will leave work two hours earlier than Daniel O'Leary.

5) No two employees arrive and leave at the same time.

Part C   Read the directions in the box and imagine that they are oral directions. Then write down the key words or ideas on a piece of paper. The words should be what you would need in order to remember the directions.

> "Here are some things to remember about using this grill. First, wipe it with cooking oil before you turn it on. Set it at middle high for everything but fried potatoes. Set it at high for them. Every time you cook something, scrape the grill with the scraper and reoil the grill. Cook onions over in the far-left corner of the grill. That way they won't make everything else smell. When the crowd ends and you have a break in the cooking, turn the grill down to medium low. If you turn it lower than that, it will take too long to heat back up if a customer comes in. When you leave at the end of the day, you make sure that the grill is clean, and I mean clean!"

Part D   Number your paper 1 to 10. Use your notes from Part C to write short answers to these questions.

1) What should you do before cooking anything?
2) At what temperature should you cook eggs?
3) What should the first temperature setting of the day be?
4) At what temperature should you make fried potatoes?
5) How often should you reoil the grill?
6) Why should you cook onions in the far-left corner of the grill?
7) If you turn the grill down too low, what will happen when a customer comes in?
8) Whose responsibility is it to clean the grill?
9) What do you have to do each time you cook something?
10) At what setting should you put the grill after the lunch crowd has gone?

Test Taking Tip   Always pay special attention to key words in a set of directions—words such as *first, second, third* or *most important, least important, all,* or *none.*

Chapter
9

Learning More Job Skills

The more skills you have, the more valuable you will be as an employee. For example, understanding how to read and use trade manuals will keep you up-to-date on the latest information in various trades.

In Chapter 9, you will learn not only how to use trade manuals but also how to interpret charts, graphs, and labels.

Goals for Learning

▶ To understand the importance of trade manuals

▶ To be able to use an index

▶ To learn to read charts, graphs, and labels

Jimmie Eagle had been working on his job for six months. He liked the work and was doing well. Because he got along so well with his supervisors and coworkers, his bosses decided that they would give him a promotion. The new job that they wanted Jimmie to take would mean that he would have to use **trade manuals** and be able to read all kinds of graphs, charts, and labels. Jimmie was glad for the promotion, but he was a little worried because he wasn't sure he would know how to do everything on the new job.

> **Trade manuals**
>
> *Handbooks explaining a particular skilled job.*

Jimmie decided to discuss his concerns with his boss. Immediately Mr. Hernandez said, "Oh, Jimmie, don't worry. We plan to send you to school for the first week you are in the new job. There you can learn everything that you will need to know." Jimmie was relieved. The school, which was held right at the factory, was run by supervisors who knew exactly what Jimmie needed to know to do a good job.

The first thing Jimmie learned was how to use, read, and understand trade manuals. Trade manuals are books about certain skilled jobs like plumbing or electrical work. They explain such things as how to do certain jobs, and they even describe new tools, methods, and products in the trade.

The company Jimmie worked for was a plumbing company. This is a section of a plumbing trade manual about water heaters that Jimmie was given to read.

The acceptable temperature for domestic hot water is from 140 to 160 degrees Fahrenheit. If an automatic clothes washer or dishwasher is in use, 160 degrees is preferred. Temperatures above 160 degrees are not recommended. They cause increased corrosion, increased deposit of lime, waste of fuel, more rapid heat loss by radiation as well as danger of scalding and other accidents.

As you were reading, you probably realized that this was information meant for a plumber who is installing a water heater. Notice that plumbers have several questions to consider when they decide the correct temperature.

- Does this family have a clothes washer?
- Does this family have a dishwasher?

Activity A   Number your paper 1 to 8. Then after you read this section of a trade manual, write short answers to the questions.

Globe valves have a machined seat and a composition disc that usually shut off tightly. However, gate valves may leak slightly when closed, particularly if frequently operated. The leaking is caused by wear between the brass gates and the faces against which they operate. Globe valves create more flow resistance than gate valves.

1) Which valve will shut off more tightly?

2) What causes a gate valve to leak?

3) Which valve creates more flow resistance?

4) Suppose that you were Jimmie and you had to pick a valve for a job. If you did not want any leaking, which valve would you choose?

5) Which valve has a machined seat and a composition disc?

6) Why do you think that frequent operation would cause a gate valve to leak?

7) Suppose that you were Jimmie and you had to pick a valve for a job. If you want the least flow resistance possible, which valve would you choose?

8) What two kinds of valves are compared in this section of the trade manual?

Manuals Describing New Materials

The next section from a trade manual describes new plumbing products. As you read it, decide if Jimmie should or should not recommend this product.

The new Rxt supply valves, manufactured by P. J. Plumbing Co., are available in both straight and angle configurations. They adapt to copper tubing, as well as plastic tubing and conventional flexible chrome-plated copper supply tubes. The compression-type connections can be installed without the use of wrenches; they represent a vast improvement over conventional brass supply valves.

235

Activity B   Number your paper 1 to 7. If a statement is true, write *True* next to the number. If it is not true, write *False*.

1) These new supply valves are manufactured by the Rxt Supply Company.

2) You can get these new valves for straight or for angled shapes.

3) They will not adapt to copper tubing.

4) They will adapt to plastic tubing.

5) You need a wrench to install these valves.

6) The new Rxt supply valves are much better than brass supply valves.

7) The P. J. Plumbing Company, which manufactures the Rxt supply valve, makes the valves in two shapes.

Index

A list of items that are found in a book with page numbers where those items can be found; an index is usually found in the back of a book.

Jimmie found that in order to get the best use from a trade manual or other instructional books, he had to know how to use an **index**. One evening when he was reading about valves in a trade manual, he turned to the index at the back of the book because he wanted more information. This is what he found in the index.

> Valve seat dresser, 7, 10
>
> Valve seat wrench, 7, 10
>
> Valves, 4, 26

If he wanted information specifically about supply valves, for example, he would try page 4 and page 26.

Major headings

The most important items in a list.

Activity A   Number your paper 1 to 5. Then write short answers to the following questions about this sample index. (Some indexes use capital letters to indicate **major headings**. Major headings are usually typed against the left margin.)

> Aluminum welding, 66–67
> Arbor press, 498
> Arc welding, 71–80
>   accessories, 73–74
>   electrode classification, 71
>   electrodes, 71
>   freezing of the electrode, 75–76
>   machines, 74
>   operations and uses, 72–74
>   protection equipment, 73
>   starting the arc, 75–77
> Arcing, 534–545

1) What two kinds of welding can you find in the book?

2) Are arcing and arc welding the same thing? How can you tell?

3) Do you need protection equipment for arc welding?

4) On what pages would you find out how to start the arc?

5) Is *electrode classification* a major heading in this index?

Activity B Number your paper 1 to 10. Then write short answers to the following questions about this sample index.

> Applications, 326–366
>   credit, 345
>   educational, 328, 347
>   financial, 365
>   job, 333
>   permits, 357
>   work benefits, 360
> Area codes, 214–218
> Catalogs, 127–198
>   business, 134
>   mail order, 144–168

1) How many major headings are included in this sample index? What are they?

2) If you wanted to find out something about an application for a building permit, on which page would you look?

3) If you wanted to find out what area codes were and how they are used, on which pages would you look?

4) If you were applying for a credit card and wanted some help filling out the application, on what page would you look?

5) If you wanted some information about ordering from a mail order catalog, on what pages would you look?

6) In order to get information about using business catalogs, on what page would you look?

7) Does this book appear to have information in it about using an atlas?

8) If you wanted to fill in an application for college, where in this book would you look?

9) If you need help filling out an application for a bank loan, on which page of this book would you look?

10) In this book, are there more pages about educational applications or about mail order catalogs? How do you know?

Chart

A diagram that presents information in a visual form.

Being able to read and interpret graphs and **charts** was another important part of Jimmie's new job. He had to be able to understand production charts, quota charts, and other work-related charts. A chart is a diagram that presents information in table or list form.

One of the charts that Jimmie had to read each month was the production chart. This chart was especially important because it identified how much each shop produced each month.

Production Chart — March, 2001			
Section	**Deluxe Model**	**Budget Model**	**Hotel and Office Model**
Bathtubs	146	278	539
Toilets	512	1,036	5,427
Sinks	448	795	968
Showers	90	40	720
	For all of the above listed:		
Fittings	1,196	2,149	7,654

On this chart each section is named for the product that it produces: bathtubs, toilets, etc. Notice that the company makes three models of each product: deluxe, budget, and one for hotels and offices. The fittings section makes all the additional parts (handles, drains, etc.) for all models of all products.

Activity A Number your paper 1 to 5. Then write short answers to these questions.

1) According to the chart, how many deluxe bathtubs were made?

2) How many showers were made?

3) How many budget model sinks were made in March?

4) Which item did Jimmie's company produce the most of in March?

5) Why does the fittings section have to know what all the other sections are doing?

Bar graph

A diagram that uses lines and shaded areas to present and compare information.

Bar Graphs

A **bar graph** is a diagram that uses lines and shaded areas to present and compare information. The following graph shows the percentage of products sent back to the company because they were faulty. The company wants to improve this record.

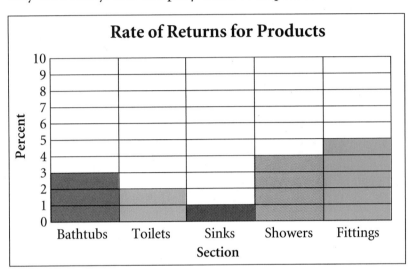

Jimmie noticed that the sinks section had the fewest returns and that fittings had the most returns. Since the fittings section had to work with the smallest parts and with the most working parts, the large number of returns made sense.

Activity B Number your paper 1 to 5. If the statement is true, write *True* next to the number. If the statement is not true, write *False*.

1) The sinks section had less than a 1% rate of return.

2) The shower section had a 4% return rate.

3) The tub section had a 20% return rate.

4) The fittings section had the most merchandise returned.

5) This graph could show a 10% rate of return.

Labels

Words or abbreviations attached to objects in order to identify or describe them.

Part of Jimmie's new job included getting stock from the stockroom. At the training program, the instructors taught him how to read and interpret the **labels** on packages so that he could tell that he was getting exactly what he needed. Labels are words or abbreviations attached to objects in order to identify or describe them.

First, Jimmie had to learn the names of the stock in the stockroom. Then he had to learn the abbreviations most commonly found on the labels on the stock. These abbreviations dealt with size, number, material, and color.

Jimmie learned the abbreviations on box labels in the stockroom.

The stockroom held hundreds of different items. Knowing the meanings of the words and abbreviations without having to look at a list helped Jimmie to find items in the stockroom quickly and easily.

When Jimmie was sent to the stockroom to get a gr. of lg. wh. plas. drain plugs, he had to know he was to get a gross of large, white, plastic drain plugs. He also had to know that there are 12 dozen in a gross. He used the following list as he was learning the most important abbreviations used in the stockroom.

Label Abbreviations

Size

sm.—small

med.—medium

lg.—large

Number

doz.—dozen

gr.—gross (12 dozen)

rm.—ream (500 sheets)

Material

st.—steel

cop.—copper

plas.—plastic

pap.—paper

Color

blk.—black

wh.—white

yel.—yellow

Activity A Number your paper 1 to 5. Then rewrite these labels by changing each abbreviation to the word it stands for.

1) Plas. Tubing sm. 2 doz. lengths wh.

2) Pap. Wallboard 1 gr. yel.

3) St. Pipe med. 3 doz.

4) Cop. Wires sm. 1 doz. yel.

5) Lg. wh. Paper 3 rm.

Many jobs require that workers be able to read and understand trade manuals. Some trade manuals explain how to do a job or how to follow a procedure. Others tell you about new products that may be better than the ones you are using. Some of these manuals are very technical and describe special trades and skills. They also often include specific language used for a particular trade. Therefore, you should always read trade manuals slowly and carefully to make sure you understand them. After all, your job may depend on it.

In order to use a trade manual as completely as possible, you need to be able to read and understand an index. An index, which is usually at the back of a book, tells you the pages on which you can find certain information. Some jobs also require that you read and understand graphs and charts. Charts and graphs provide information in a quick, easy-to-see way. Another important aspect of some jobs is the ability to read and understand labels.

While all of the above skills vary from job to job, it is important that you are familiar with all of them—just in case a new job requires using one or all of them.

Part A   Number your paper 1 to 5. Then after you read this entry from a trade manual, write short answers to the following questions.

Directions to Set an Electrical Timer

Slide one control tab completely out, toward the edge of the dial, for each hour of "on" time you want. Sliding out a tab between 5:00 P.M. and 6:00 P.M. will turn on an appliance for one hour, beginning at 5:00 P.M. If you desire a longer period of time, slide out additional control tabs.

1) What are these directions for?
2) If you slide one control tab out, how long will the appliance operate?
3) In which direction should the tab be pushed to be "out"?
4) If you want the appliance to run for more than one hour, what should you do?
5) If you slide out the tabs between 9:00 P.M. and 11:00 P.M., how long will the timer be on?

Part B   Number your paper 1 to 10. Then write short answers to the following questions that are based on this sample index.

Counters, 74–90
  building, 74–80
  installation,
    80–85
  measurement,
    74–78
  tops, 85–90
Drains, 55–73
  appliance, 72
  fixture, 55–60
  floor, 60
  unstopping,
    61–64

1) Does this book give information on installing counters?
2) On what pages would you look to find out about measuring counters?
3) If you wanted to build a counter yourself, on what pages would you look?
4) What three kinds of drains are discussed in this book?
5) What pages would you read if you wanted to study the whole section on drains?
6) On what pages would you look if you wanted to find out how to unstop a drain?
7) If you wanted to replace a countertop, where would you look?
8) On what page would you look to find information on different kinds of drains used in various fixtures?
9) How many pages cover information on countertops?
10) Which section comes first in the book: counters or drains?

Part C   Number your paper 1 to 5. Then write the word from the box that completes each statement. (Use each answer only once.)

products	index	do
manuals	procedures	

1) Trade _____ are books about certain jobs or skills.

2) They give instructions on how to _____ certain jobs.

3) Sometimes they explain how to follow new _____ .

4) They can also describe new _____ .

5) If you look in the _____ , you will find page numbers where you can find information on specific topics.

Part D   Number your paper 1 to 5. Then match each term in the first column with its meaning or explanation in the second column.

Term

1) charts
2) labels
3) bar graphs
4) abbreviations
5) major headings

Meaning

a) diagrams that use lines and shaded areas to present and compare information

b) the most important items in a list

c) the shortened forms of written words

d) words or abbreviations attached to objects in order to identify or describe them

e) diagrams that present information in table or list form

Test Taking Tip   When studying for a test, review any tests or quizzes you took earlier that cover the same information.

Chapter 10

Filling Out Business Forms

Many jobs require that you know how to complete a certain amount of paperwork. Whether you have to fill out sales slips or write order letters, it is important that you are accurate. This chapter will help you gain confidence in these areas.

In Chapter 10, you will review different kinds of forms that you will have to fill out in some companies. You will also learn how to use catalogs to write order letters, and you will learn how to write a follow-up letter when an order is wrong.

Goals for Learning

▶ To learn how to fill out sales slips and invoices

▶ To be able to use computer printouts to maintain a company's inventory and to know when to reorder items

▶ To know how to use catalogs to reorder merchandise

▶ To learn how to write an order letter

▶ To be able to write a follow-up letter

George Hill is a sales clerk for Value Office Supplies, which has five stores in Memphis, Tennessee. In the main store on South Street, George sells office supplies to walk-in customers, and he also takes phone orders.

George's friend, Wilma Brown, works for the same company in the stock department. She works with the **inventory** in all five stores and with the inventory in the warehouse. She lists the amount of goods or materials on hand and makes sure that each store has enough of the right items. During the course of each day, both George and Wilma have to fill out several kinds of forms. Wilma also has to write letters to order stock items and to follow up on orders.

George has to fill out a **sales slip** every time a customer buys supplies. He keeps a copy of this form so that the company has a record of who bought what, how much they paid, and when they made the purchase. Here is a sample of the sales slip that George has to complete for each sale.

Inventory

The amount of goods and materials on hand; stock.

Sales slip

A form used by retail stores as a record of a purchase or sale.

Value Office Supplies
14 South Street
Memphis, Tennessee 38101

Date _March 17, 2001_

Sold to _John Murray_

Address _2736 Natchez Place_

City, State, ZIP _Memphis, TN 38113_

How Many	Item #	Description	Unit Price	Amount
5	9738	Legal pads	$5.60	$28.00
1 box	7638	Butterfly clips	4.00	4.00
1	1121	Name stamp	7.00	7.00
			Subtotal	$39.00
			Sales Tax	3.22
			Total	$42.22

Amount
On a sales slip, the product of the number purchased times the unit price.

Item number
The figure used to identify each separate item sold by a company; used in inventory lists, in catalogs, on sales slips, etc.

Sales tax
A tax figured as a percentage of the cost of the sale and collected by the company that sells the goods.

Subtotal
The sum of part of a series of figures; on a sales slip, the sum of the amounts of various items purchased before the sales tax is added.

Total
On a sales slip, the sales tax is added to the subtotal to give the total amount of the purchase.

Unit price
The cost for one item, box, dozen, gallon, pound, etc.

Notice how neatly and carefully George filled out the sales slip with the date, customer's name, address, city, and ZIP code. Below that information are five columns. The first column asks, "How many?" The second column asks for an **item number** that identifies each separate item sold by the company. George can find that number from the label on the item or from a catalog printed by his company. Then, in the third column, he described what the item is.

He wrote the price for each item in the fourth column. That column contains the price of only one unit of each item. Sometimes this **unit price** is not just for each single item but rather for each box, each dozen, each gallon, etc. Because Mr. Murray bought five packages of legal pads, George had to multiply $5.60 by 5 (the unit price times the number purchased) to get the **amount** in the last column. The cost for five pads, therefore, was $28.00. Since Mr. Murray bought only one box of butterfly clips and one name stamp, George did not have to multiply to get those amounts. After George listed everything Mr. Murray had bought, he added the amounts in the last column to get the **subtotal** of $39.00.

In Memphis, customers have to pay an 8.25% **sales tax** on goods they buy. As a result, George had to figure the amount for sales tax by multiplying the subtotal of $39.00 by 8.25%. He found that the sales tax for this order came to $3.22. Finally, he added the subtotal and the tax to get a final **total** of $42.22 for Mr. Murray's bill.

George told Wilma that he always checks his math twice to make sure that all sales slips are correct. He also checks to make sure that he has copied the item numbers correctly. He added, "A sales slip is an important record for the store and for the customer, but an incorrect sales slip can make customers angry and can cost the company money."

Activity A Number your paper 1 to 14. Then list the 14 mistakes made in filling out this sales slip.

Value Office Supplies
14 South Street
Memphis, Tennessee 38101

Date _____

Sold to _Wolanski_____

Address _Calhoun Ave._____

City, State, ZIP _Memphis_____

How Many	Item #	Description	Unit Price	Amount
3	9711	Typing paper		$12.51
6		Correction fluid	1.00	6.00
2	8321			7.00
4	9101	Memo pads	1.25	6.00
3	4320	Liquid adhesive	3.00	9.15
			Subtotal	$50.76
			Sales Tax	3.93
			Total	$54.85

Lesson 2   Invoices

Invoice

A form containing a list of the goods sold; some invoices also have the price of each item and the conditions of the sale.

George also has to fill out **invoices**. An invoice, which is similar to a sales slip, contains a list of goods sold. It gives the price of each item and the terms of sale. George uses an invoice for customers who have accounts with Value Office Supplies. These customers pay a monthly bill rather than paying for each sale. On page 161 is a sample of an invoice George filled out.

Value Office Supplies

- Office Supplies
- Printing
- Office Furniture

14 South Street
Memphis, Tennessee 38101

D
E
L
I   **TO**
V
E
R

If delivery address is different from shown below, fill in above

B
I   **TO**   Franklin N. Brussells
L   2345 Beech Street
L   Memphis, Tennessee 38024

Invoice Number	591006
Date	4 - 1 - 01
Customer Order Number	37 - 24
Ordered by	Smith
Sold by	Hill
Audit	

✓	Quantity Ordered	Quantity Delivered	Unit of Sale	Description	Unit Price	Per	Amount
	2	2	dz.	948 Pads	$12.00	dz.	$24.00
					Subtotal		$24.00

Service Charge of 1½% per month, 18% per annum, will be applied to all 60 day old balances.

Received above items in good condition

Regular stock merchandise can be returned for exchange credit or refund if in perfect condition and if returned within 30 days of date of purchase.

| Sales Tax | 1.98 |
| Total | $25.98 |

On the top left side of this invoice, there is a space for the name and address of the person or company who bought the goods. There is also space for George to write a delivery address if it is different from the billing address. (The directions say, "If delivery address is different from shown below, fill in above.")

On the right side, there is the invoice number, which is always printed on the form. Below that there is a place for the date, customer order number, name of the person who ordered goods, and name of the salesperson who made the sale. Then it is George's responsibility to list information about the ordered items on the appropriate lines.

One copy of the invoice goes to the customer for his or her personal or company's records, and another copy is kept by the salesperson. The third copy goes to the billing department, and the last copy goes to the inventory department.

In many companies today, computers do most of the work involved with invoices. Instead of writing out invoices, an employee types in all of the information into a computer. Then the computer prints out the invoice.

Activity A   Number your paper 1 to 10. Then write short answers to the following questions about this invoice.

• Office Supplies • Printing • Office Furniture		**Value Office Supplies** 14 South Street Memphis, Tennessee 38101				

DELIVER TO: Standard Wharf, 11 Murphy Street, 38170

If delivery address is different from shown below, fill in above

BILL TO: Standard Company, 4627 Dale Street, 38181

Invoice Number	591038
Date	5 - 6 - 01
Customer Order Number	4961
Ordered by	Brad
Sold by	Hill
Audit	

✓	Quantity Ordered	Quantity Delivered	Unit of Sale	Description	Unit Price	Per	Amount
	1	1	ea.	B64 Desk	$175.15	ea.	$175.15
✓	2	1	ea.	N77 Desk Chair	45.00	ea.	90.00
✓	Other chair will follow				Subtotal		$265.15

Service Charge of 1½% per month, 18% per annum, will be applied to all 60 day old balances.

Received above items in good condition

Regular stock merchandise can be returned for exchange credit or refund if in perfect condition and if returned within 30 days of date of purchase.

Sales Tax	21.88
Total	$287.03

1) Where was the furniture delivered?

2) Why was the furniture delivered to some place other than where the bill was sent?

3) Who ordered the furniture?

4) How many desks were ordered and delivered?

5) Which salesperson made the sale?

6) How much did the desk cost?

7) How many chairs were ordered and delivered?

8) How much did each chair cost?

9) What was the total cost for the chairs?

10) Why do you think that only one chair was delivered?

After George and the other salespeople fill out sales slips, copies are sent to Wilma's department. She and her coworkers check off what items have been sold from the inventory. An inventory is a list of what goods or materials a company like Value Office Supplies has on hand. When sold items are subtracted from the inventory, the workers know what items are left in stock and what inventory items may be running low.

When the number of any item is low in the inventory, the people in Wilma's office know that it may be time to reorder that item. The number that indicates it is time to reorder is decided ahead of time. To make the decision, Wilma uses the history of the item's sales. This record tells how many of the item sells each month of the year and shows the times of year that the item sells best. How long it will take to get more of the item is also a factor in deciding the right time to reorder. The company does not want to run out of stock.

Value Office Supplies, like most other businesses, uses computers to keep its inventory. Keeping track of the inventory by computer is easy and exact. Every day as copies of the sales slips arrive in her office, Wilma enters the items that have been sold into the computer. If she needs to know which store is selling how much of what, a **computer printout** can tell her. (A sample computer printout is shown on page 164.)

Computer printout

A printed record produced automatically by a computer.

For example, on March 17, 2001, when George sold John Murray one box of butterfly clips, Wilma entered that item into the computer. Since George works at the main store, that box of clips was included in the total number of boxes of clips the main store sold that day.

```
BOXES SOLD
BUTTERFLY CLIPS
    DATE        MAIN STORE      PLAZA      3RD ST.      OPERA      FINE ST.
    3/15           92             5          12           8           7
    3/16           56             4          10          11           6
    3/17           71            10           5           9           3
```

This computer printout tells how many boxes of butterfly clips were sold in each of the five stores for three days. Included in the 71 boxes sold at the main store on March 17 is the one box that George sold to Mr. Murray.

Once these figures are entered into the computer, Wilma has the information she needs to determine if the company's stock of butterfly clips is low enough to reorder.

```
ITEM:    BUTTERFLY CLIPS                    REORDER BELOW: 500 BOXES
3/10        IN STOCK - 1,050 BOXES
3/13        TO MAIN STORE - 510 BOXES
            REMAINDER - 540 BOXES
3/14        TO PLAZA STORE - 35 BOXES
            REMAINDER - 505 BOXES
3/14        TO 3RD ST. STORE - 10 BOXES
            REMAINDER - 495 BOXES              REORDER
3/14        ORDERED 2,016
3/21        RECEIVED ORDER
            TOTAL - 2,511
```

Wilma can tell from the information on the computer that on March 10, the company had 1,050 boxes of butterfly clips on hand in the warehouse. Because the main store was getting low on butterfly clips, she sent it 510 boxes on March 13. The next day, she also sent the Plaza Store 35 boxes and the 3rd Street Store 10 boxes. These figures meant that only 495 boxes of butterfly clips were left in inventory in the warehouse.

Next to the figure *495* on the printout, the computer printed the word *REORDER* because at the top of the printout, there are instructions to reorder when the supply gets "Below 500 boxes." Therefore, on March 14, Wilma ordered 2,016 boxes of butterfly clips. The printout states that she received the order on March 21.

Activity A Number your paper 1 to 6. Then write short answers to the following questions about this computer printout about the inventory of correction fluid.

```
ITEM: CORRECTION FLUID          REORDER BELOW: 30 DOZ. BOT.
3/10        IN STOCK - 76 DOZEN BOT.
3/10        TO FINE ST. STORE - 10 DOZ. BOT.
            REMAINDER - 66 DOZ. BOT.
3/14        TO OPERA STORE - 12 DOZ. BOT.
            REMAINDER - 54 DOZ. BOT.
3/15        TO MAIN STORE - 20 DOZ. BOT.
            REMAINDER - 34 DOZ. BOT.
```

1) Did Wilma have to reorder correction fluid from March 10 through March 15? Why or why not?

2) How many bottles of correction fluid were in stock at the close of the day on March 10?

3) Why do you think there is no entry for March 13?

4) How many bottles of correction fluid were sent to the main store? When were they sent?

5) How many bottles of correction fluid were in stock at the close of the day on March 15?

6) When do you think Wilma will probably need to reorder correction fluid? Explain your answer.

Catalog

A listing of items arranged in a systematic way; a description of these items is often included.

When Wilma had to reorder butterfly clips, she used the **catalog** put out by the paper-clip company. She had to read the catalog descriptions to tell which kind of clip she wanted. She was careful that she didn't make a mistake because mistakes cause delays that might result in the stores' not having enough butterfly clips to sell to their own customers.

Here is the section of the catalog that Wilma used to make her order. In this order, the unit price is for each gross, not each box. (There are twelve dozen boxes, or 144 boxes, in a gross.)

Clips

#5566 – paper	100 per box	**$5.78** per gross
#5567 – paper	500 per box	**$20.11** per gross
#5580 – butterfly	50 per box	**$4.90** per gross
#5581 – butterfly	100 per box	**$9.20** per gross

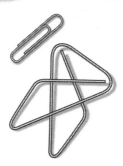

Because Wilma knew that the clips she wanted came 100 per box, she reordered item #5581.

If Wilma had ordered item #5566, she would have received regular paper clips—like the top drawing. They would not have been what the stores needed. Instead, she ordered item #5581, the butterfly clips—like the bottom drawing. Apparently, most of Value Office Supplies' customers had needed paperclips that held greater amounts of paper than regular paperclips.

Activity A   Number your paper 1 to 8. If the following statements about this catalog entry are true, write *True* next to the number. If the statements are not true, write *False*.

Pens

Ballpoint,	throwaway	$7.70 doz.
Ballpoint,	refillable	$11.55 doz.
Ballpoint,	retractable throwaway.....	$10.45 doz.
Ballpoint,	retractable refillable.......	$14.33 doz.

1) Four kinds of ballpoint pens are listed in this catalog entry.

2) The lowest price is for throwaway pens with retractable points.

3) You cannot buy refillable pens that do not have retractable points.

4) Refillable pens with retractable points are the most expensive pens.

5) Businesses that provide pens for their employees and/or customers would probably buy throwaway pens without retractable points because they have the lowest price.

6) Two dozen ballpoint pens with retractable points that cannot be refilled cost $24.90.

7) The throwaway ballpoint pens without retractable tips cost about 64¢ each.

8) The refillable ballpoint pens with retractable tips cost about $1.19 each.

Order letters

Letters written to order merchandise from a company.

Fax machine

A machine for sending copies of printed pages over telephone lines.

Part of Wilma's job is writing **order letters** to order merchandise. Not all items are ordered by mail. Some rush orders are made over the telephone or by **fax machine**. However, some businesses prefer to order by fax because letters give them a record of what they have ordered and when it was ordered. If companies receive the wrong items, they can simply refer to their copy of the letter to prove that they did not make the error.

Wilma uses the fax machine to send many order letters.

Because letters ordering merchandise are so important, Wilma is careful to include all the information needed to receive the correct items. When she ordered butterfly clips, for example, she followed the directions listed below when she wrote the body of her order letter.

1. An order letter must include the billing/shipping address of the company.

2. The item number from the catalog must appear in the order letter.

3. Along with each item number, include a description of the item.

4. Write the unit, or individual price, of each item.

5. Include the number of units being ordered.

6. Find the subtotal for the units, figure the amount of the sales tax, and add the subtotal of the units and the sales tax. Write the total cost for the order.

7. State the way in which Value Office Supplies will pay for the merchandise.

8. Indicate the preferred delivery method.

9. Write the date when the merchandise should be delivered.

If Wilma leaves any of this information out of her order letter, the order may take longer to get. Worse yet, Wilma might not get the right order. For example, if Wilma included the item description and no item number, the company might send her something different from what she wanted.

Taking the time to include all of the necessary information in an order letter can save time and money in the end.

Activity A   On your paper, list any information Wilma left out of this order letter. (Use the list on page 169 to help you.)

Value Office Supplies
14 South Street
Memphis, Tennessee 38101

March 14, 2001

Mr. Robert Michael
Arlington Clip Company
6500 Wright Avenue
Trenton, NJ 08608

Dear Mr. Michael:

Please ship to the above address 14 gross of butterfly clips, 100 per box, at a cost of $9.20 per gross.

Thank you for your cooperation.

Sincerely,

Wilma Brown

Wilma Brown
Stock Department

Activity B   On your paper, write a letter ordering 10 dozen reams of erasable bond paper, measuring $8\frac{1}{2}''$ by $11''$. Make up the name and address of the company from which you are ordering. Add any other needed information to your letter. At the end, request that the company send you a bill. (Use the list on page 169 to help you.)

No matter how careful Wilma and her coworkers are, sometimes a mistake is made in an order. Sometimes the order contains the wrong merchandise or does not include the right amount. Even worse, sometimes the order never arrives. If any of these mistakes are made, Wilma has to write a **follow-up letter**. This kind of letter should explain the problem clearly and politely. It should also spell out what the company wants done to correct the mistake.

Follow-up letter

A second letter written to correct a mistake, to give or ask for additional information, or to suggest solutions to a problem.

When Wilma writes a follow-up letter, she always includes some of the information she included in the earlier order letter—as well as some new information. She follows the directions listed below when she writes the body of her follow-up letter.

1. A follow-up letter must include the item number from the catalog.

2. A description of the item is helpful in a follow-up letter.

3. List the unit, or individual price, of each item.

4. Include the total of the number of units ordered.

5. Include the subtotal of the units, the sales tax, and the total cost.

6. Provide copies of the necessary bills, invoices, or other information.

7. Explain the problem.

8. Think about the steps needed to solve this problem and include them in your follow-up letter.

Wilma always carefully checks the rough drafts of her follow-up letters to make sure that all the information in the letters is correct. It is just as important for a follow-up letter to be correct as it is for an order letter to be correct.

Activity A On your paper, list any information Wilma left out of this follow-up letter. (Use the list on page 171 to help you.)

Value Office Supplies
14 South Street
Memphis, Tennessee 38101

March 23, 2001

Mr. Robert Michael
Arlington Clip Company
6500 Wright Avenue
Trenton, NJ 08608

Dear Mr. Michael:

On March 14, I ordered from your company 14 gross of butterfly clips, 100 per box, at the cost of $9.20 per gross. The item number for those clips is #5581.

On March 21, I received from you 14 gross of butterfly clips, 50 per box, for which Value Office Supplies was charged $9.20 per gross. Attached is a copy of the invoice sent with this order.

Please send us the correct merchandise immediately. Credit our account for the original order that we shipped back to you today. We must have the correct order by March 31 in order to keep enough stock in our inventory.

I would appreciate your immediate attention to this matter.

Sincerely,

Wilma Brown

Wilma Brown
Stock Department

Two of the most frequently used business forms are the sales slip and the invoice. These forms must be filled out carefully in order to give both the customer and the company accurate information about what was bought when and how much was paid for it. Many companies use computers to complete these forms, but some do not.

Sales slips and invoices are used to help companies keep track of inventory. A well-kept inventory makes it possible for companies never to run out of the important items they need to operate their businesses.

Sometime in the future, you may work at a job that requires you to order supplies and equipment for your company. If that happens, you will also need to know how to use order catalogs.

If you are in charge of ordering supplies, you will find it helpful to know what business-letter forms are and what information should be included in an order letter. When incorrect orders arrive, you must also know how to write a good follow-up letter that explains what the problem is and how the problem should be corrected.

Being able to fill out forms correctly, to read computer printouts, and to write good letters are skills that are important in many jobs. Knowing these skills can make you a valued employee.

Part A   Number your paper 1 to 5. Then write short answers to the following questions about this entry from a supply catalog.

Paper—8¹/₂ × 11

Bond, erasable .... **$15.00** per ream
Bond, nonerasable .... **$12.25** per ream
Bond, ripple erasable .... **$18.00** per ream

1) How many different kinds of paper are listed in this entry? What size is all of the paper?

2) How much does one ream of ripple erasable bond paper cost?

3) What is the least expensive kind of paper in this entry?

4) If you wanted to purchase ten reams of nonerasable bond, how much would it cost?

5) If you ordered two reams of nonerasable bond and four reams of ripple erasable bond, what would your total bill be?

Part B   On your paper, write an order letter to Phillips Paper Company. Order 7 reams of $8\frac{1}{2}$″ by 11″ ripple erasable bond paper that costs $18.00 per ream. Phillips Paper Company is located on 115 Howard Street, Newark, DE 19711. You are enclosing a check for the total cost of the paper. You do not have to pay sales tax. Add any other information needed to make this order letter complete. (Check the list Wilma used to write her order letter on page 169.)

Part C The Phillips Paper Company sent you 7 reams of $8 \frac{1}{2}''$ by $14''$ erasable bond paper instead of what you ordered in Part B. Write a follow-up letter explaining the company's mistake and explaining what you want done to correct it. Add any other information needed to make this follow-up letter complete. (Check the list Wilma used to write her follow-up letter on page 171.)

Part D Number your paper 1 to 10. If the statement is true, write *True* next to the number. If the statement is not true, write *False*.

1) Because you write the remaining inventory on a sales slip, sales slips help to keep inventory records up to date.

2) An invoice often includes more information than a sales slip.

3) An order letter is a good record of exactly what was ordered and when it was ordered.

4) Merchandise from a catalog can only be ordered by phone or fax.

5) A follow-up letter never repeats information from an order letter.

6) An incomplete sales slip may cause problems with keeping an accurate inventory.

7) In a follow-up letter, you should always state that the mistake causes your company serious problems.

8) If sales slips are not figured correctly, only the customer can get cheated.

9) From a computer printout, you can automatically learn when it is time to reorder an item.

10) A computer printout contains copies of all invoices.

| Test Taking Tip | Do not wait until the night before a test to study. Plan your study time so that you can get a good night's sleep the night before a test. |

Communicating With the Public

M ost jobs today require some form of communication. For example, employees may have to greet customers, answer the telephone, or attend meetings. What you say and how you say it will often determine how successful you will be at your job.

In Chapter 11, you will become familiar with various work situations that require good communication skills. Then you will see how knowing what to say and what to write can help you handle all of these situations with confidence.

Goals for Learning

▶ To understand the correct way to answer a telephone call

▶ To learn how to take helpful telephone messages and transfer calls

▶ To understand how a business meeting is conducted and how to take minutes at a meeting

▶ To recognize the elements of a good business letter to customers, and to be able to write one

Hector Rosario works as a clerk for Smith, Marchi, and Glassman, a small insurance company. One of his most important duties is talking and writing to the company's customers. He makes sure that customers get to talk to the right people so that they get their questions answered. He also answers all letters that request general information from the company.

Mr. Smith has told Hector that his job is very important because he is often the first person to talk to or correspond with new customers. In fact, whether or not Hector makes a good impression can sometimes make all the difference between getting a new customer or not. As a result, the company's partners were very careful when they promoted him to his current position. They knew they needed someone who was a good communicator—someone who could do a good job talking and writing to customers.

Everyone at the company is very pleased with the job Hector has done. The company is growing fast, and Hector's job has become too big for one person. Because of Hector's good work, his supervisor has asked him to train Yuki Kono to help him.

Yuki speaks politely, uses English well, and has a pleasant personality. It's up to Hector now to teach Yuki how to do the rest of the job.

The first thing that Hector felt Yuki should know about was the correct way to answer the telephone. He told her that her voice and manner would be the first impression many people had of the company, and the company wanted that impression to be a good one. "An unpleasant tone in your voice can make customers decide that they will buy their insurance from someone else," explained Hector. "It's a good idea to imagine people's faces when you answer the phone, and it's your job to make those faces smile. You want people to feel comfortable and to know that we want their business."

Listed below, you will find eight tips that Hector gave Yuki about using the telephone.

1. Pick up the phone after the first or second ring. Being slow to answer the phone may make customers feel that the company doesn't care about them.

2. Be pleasant and sincere.

3. After you give the name of the company, give your own name. For example, you would say, "Smith, Marchi, and Glassman Insurance Company. Yuki Kono speaking."

4. Listen carefully. Nothing is more annoying to customers than being asked to repeat what they said because you weren't listening.

5. Always be polite, friendly, and helpful. Even if a customer is unpleasant, remain friendly and cooperative. Never get nasty or rude.

6. Take accurate and complete **messages**. Also, make sure that the messages get to the right people as soon as possible.

7. End a call by making the customer feel that you care about what was said, that you will do everything necessary to take care of any problem, and that you were glad to be able to help.

8. Always let the customers hang up first so that you can be sure that they have said everything they want to say.

Message

A written or a spoken form of communication.

Yuki thanked Hector for the eight hints and promised to remember all of them. She wanted to answer the telephone correctly because she knew that good telephone manners are important to her company. She set a goal for herself. Every time she talked to a customer on the telephone, she would make a good impression.

Activity A Number your paper 1 to 11. Then write the word or words that complete each of these hints for good telephone manners.

1) Pick up the telephone on the _____ or _____ ring.

2) If you let the phone ring too long, it makes the customer feel that you don't _____ .

3) Be _____ and _____ .

4) When you answer the telephone, first give the _____ of your company.

5) Then give your own _____ .

6) Listen _____ .

7) Don't make customers _____ what they have already said.

8) Be polite, _____ , and _____ .

9) If the customer is _____ , remain _____ and _____ .

10) Sometimes you will have to take a _____ .

11) Make sure that it is _____ and _____ .

Activity B Number your paper 1 to 5. Then write what you would say in response to these remarks that customers might make on the telephone.

1) "What company did you say this was?"

2) "What do you mean that Ms. Singer is not available? Stop trying to give me the runaround."

3) "You make sure that Mr. Guth gets my message."

4) "My name is Mr. Kzidklsl." (The voice is unclear. You cannot understand what the person has said.)

5) "Have Ms. Singer call me at 555-9846 before three o'clock."

Activity C Number your paper 1 to 8. Then write the letter of each hint in the order in which it should be done.

a) End the call by making the customer feel that you care about what was said and that you were glad to help.

b) Be pleasant and sincere.

c) Be polite, friendly, and helpful. Even if a customer is unpleasant, remain friendly.

d) Pick up the phone after the first or second ring.

e) If you take a message, make sure that it is accurate and complete.

f) Listen carefully.

g) Let the customer hang up first.

h) First give the name of the company and then say your own name.

Yuki knows that good telephone manners will help her succeed in her new job.

Taking Care of a Customer

"These hints are not all there is to talking to people on the telephone, Yuki," warned Hector. "Once customers tell you why they are calling, you have to know what to do."

"What do you mean?" asked Yuki.

"Well," said Hector, "suppose a customer asks to speak to Mr. Smith. You can respond in several ways. For example, if Mr. Smith is in and taking calls, you can say, 'One minute, please. I'll connect you with Mr. Smith.' But what would you do if you buzz him, and he's not in his office?"

Intercom

A two-way system that has a microphone and a loudspeaker that allows people in nearby office areas to talk to each other without leaving their desks.

"I'd call him on the office **intercom**," Yuki said. "If he doesn't answer that, I would tell the customer that I cannot reach him, but I would offer to take a message."

"Good, Yuki!" exclaimed Hector. "However, never keep a customer waiting on the line for more than 10 or 15 seconds without explaining why." Hector thought for a minute and then added, "Now, suppose a customer calls and doesn't give his or her name. How would you ask for it?"

"I guess I could say, 'May I have your name, please?'" replied Yuki.

Hector said, "An even better way is to say, 'May I tell Mr. Smith who is calling?'" Then he added, "If Mr. Smith isn't in or can't be reached, here are some other things you can do."

1. You can ask if anyone else could help the customer.

2. You can offer to help the customer yourself.

3. You can offer to take a message for Mr. Smith.

Voice mail

An electronic system that records telephone messages that are played back later by the recipient.

4. If the company has a **voice mail** system, you can ask the customer if he or she wants to leave a message on Mr. Smith's voice mail.

5. You can offer to have Mr. Smith call the customer back when he returns to his office.

Activity D   Number your paper 1 to 3. Then write answers to these questions.

1) Why shouldn't you leave a customer waiting on the line for more than 10 to 15 seconds?

2) If the person the customer wants to talk to is not available, what are five things you can do?

3) Why is the person who answers the telephone so important to a company?

Activity E   On your paper, write how you would handle each of these situations. Remember that you want to make the customer happy.

Situation 1   The customer asks to speak to Mrs. Marchi, but she is out of town at a business meeting.

Situation 2   The customer asks to speak to Mr. Smith, but he is out to lunch. However, he will be back in the office at 1:30 P.M.

Situation 3   The customer is thinking about increasing her life insurance, but she wants to talk to somebody who can give her some advice. Ms. Glassman is the company expert on life insurance.

Situation 4   The customer is very angry because he thinks that the bill for his insurance premium is too high. The billing department at the company handles the bills.

Situation 5   The customer wants to talk to someone about switching his automobile insurance coverage to your company. Mrs. Marchi is the company expert on automobile insurance, but she is out of town. Mr. Smith also knows about automobile insurance.

Situation 6   John Acree, a very important customer, calls and wants to speak to anyone who is available.

Taking messages and transferring calls correctly are two important office skills.

Because Hector knew that one of the most important steps in answering telephone calls is being able to take accurate, clear, and complete messages, he gave Yuki these suggestions.

1. Keep a pad of message forms, a pen, and a pencil near the phone at all times.

2. When customers tell you who they want to speak to, write that person's name on the correct line of the message form.

3. Fill in the date and the time accurately. If the call is made at 9:15 A.M., make sure you write 9:15 A.M., not 9:00 A.M.

4. Then write the name of the person who called, what company he or she is with, and the caller's phone number and **extension**. If it is a long distance call, include the **area code**.

5. Check the appropriate box or boxes on the message form—such as TELEPHONED, CALLED TO SEE YOU, WANTS TO SEE YOU, PLEASE CALL, WILL CALL AGAIN, URGENT, or RETURNED YOUR CALL. (See the sample message form on page 185.)

6. Write any additional message the caller gives.

7. Finally, sign your name at the bottom of the form. Then the person receiving the message will know who took the call, in case there are any questions about it.

Extension

An extra telephone connection to the principal line; the number to connect to such a telephone line.

Area code

A three-digit number that identifies each telephone service area in the country.

The information on a message form should be correct. For example, if you are not sure how to spell the caller's name, ask for the correct spelling. If you had trouble hearing some information the caller gave, ask the caller to repeat it. In fact, before hanging up, it's a good idea to repeat the message to the caller to make sure you wrote everything down correctly.

This is a sample message form that Hector gave Yuki.

To: K. Smith

Date: 9/5/01   Time: 10:15 A.M.

WHILE YOU WERE OUT

Mrs. Mary Tyler

of Tyler Associates

Phone: ___–___   555-1700   36

Area Code   Number   extension

TELEPHONED	✓	PLEASE CALL	✓
CALLED TO SEE YOU		WILL CALL AGAIN	
WANTS TO SEE YOU		URGENT	
	RETURNED YOUR CALL		

Message: She needs an explanation regarding the insurance on her office.

Call taken by: Hector Rosario

Notice that the person who took the message filled in every important piece of information. It's also easy to see why clear handwriting is important. The person who reads the message needs to be able to read the names and numbers correctly.

The person who took this message was also careful to check the appropriate boxes in the middle of the form. As a result, Mr. Smith knows that he has to call Mary Tyler back. He also knows that Hector took the message, because he signed his full name at the bottom of the form.

To: _____ Joe _____

Date: _____   Time: 9:38 _____

WHILE YOU WERE OUT

M Eagles _____

of _____

Phone: _____ 555-9876 _____
         Area Code   Number   extension

TELEPHONED	PLEASE CALL	
CALLED TO SEE YOU	WILL CALL AGAIN	
WANTS TO SEE YOU	URGENT	
RETURNED YOUR CALL		

Message: wants an estimate on
                      homeowners insurance

_____

_____

Call taken by: _____

Activity B Number your paper 1 to 5. If a statement is true, write *True* next to the number. If it is not true, write *False.*

1) The only thing you have to keep by your phone to take messages is a pencil.

2) It is not important to find out the name of the caller.

3) Write all numbers carefully so that they can easily be read.

4) You don't have to bother checking any box on the message form because the person receiving the message will know what the caller wants.

5) The person getting the message doesn't have to know who took the message.

Transferring Calls

Transfer

To switch a business telephone call to another department or person.

If Hector cannot help the person who is calling, he **transfers**, or switches, that call to another department or to another person in the company. He pointed out to Yuki that transferring business calls correctly is as important as taking accurate messages.

"Do I need to say anything to the customer before I transfer the call?" asked Yuki.

"When you transfer a call," said Hector, "first explain to the caller why you are transferring the call to someone else. Then make sure that you give the caller the name and extension number of the person who will be receiving the call. That's important," he said, "because if the caller accidentally gets **disconnected**, he or she can call back and ask for the right person."

Disconnected

Not connected; a term describing a telephone connection that has been severed or ended.

Then Hector showed Yuki how to transfer a customer's call. Yuki needed to know how to use the correct method for transferring a call so that she wouldn't disconnect a caller. Finally, Hector told her to stay on the line until she is sure that the call has been transferred successfully. Hector explained that more people hang up when calls are being transferred than at any other time. As a result, transfers have to be made quickly.

Activity C Number your paper 1 to 4. Then list these steps for transferring a call in the right order. Begin with the step that you should do first.

a) Use the correct method for transferring a call.

b) Explain why you have to transfer the call.

c) Remain on the line until you know that the call has been successfully transferred.

d) Give the caller the name and extension of the person you are transferring the call to.

Minutes
Official notes taken at a meeting.

Motion
An official proposal.

Resolution
An agreed upon course of action.

Second
A statement that one agrees to or supports a motion under discussion at a meeting.

Hector told Yuki that there was another part of their job that they had not discussed yet. Every once in a while, one of the partners would ask him to sit in on a business meeting and take **minutes**.

Minutes are an official written record of what happens at a meeting. They are important because they are filed as an official record of what took place at the meeting. As a result, the person who takes the minutes has a big responsibility to take careful, accurate notes of what actually happened.

Because Yuki had never taken minutes before, she asked Hector to help her. He gave her this list of tips on how to take minutes at a meeting.

1. Take notes on anything that happens that you think is important. You can summarize a discussion, but you must take down word for word any **motions** or **resolutions** that are made. A motion is a formal call for action, or a proposal made at a meeting. For example, someone might say, "I make a motion that we spend $10,000 for advertising." A resolution is a formal statement of a decision or an expression of opinion voted by an official body or assembled group. Include the names of the people who make the motions and resolutions and the names of the people who **second** them. To second means to state that one agrees with or supports a motion under discussion.

2. If you do not understand something that is being discussed, ask someone at the meeting to explain it to you.

3. Type a final copy of the minutes as soon after the meeting as possible when everything is fresh in your mind.

4. Remember that the minutes you write must be accurate and **objective** summaries of the decisions made and the actions taken at a meeting. Include only the facts, and do not let personal feelings, prejudices, or interpretations influence you.

Hector also explained to Yuki that usually she would be given an **agenda** when she got to a meeting. An agenda is a list of topics that are going to be discussed at the meeting—in the order in which they will be discussed. He told her, "An agenda will help you follow the meeting, and later it will help you organize your notes."

Note Taking

"Write down key words and phrases that will help you remember what was discussed at a meeting," Hector advised Yuki. "In most cases, don't write down every word. Instead, summarize general discussions and debated ideas." He added, "You can also abbreviate words. For example, suppose a committee is talking about ways to get more customers, and Ms. Glassman suggests that the company advertise in the newspaper. You could write down something that looks like this."

> *Ways to get cust.*
> *Glassman — adv. in paper*

"If Mrs. Marchi suggests advertising in all the media, you could write down something that looks like this."

> *Marchi — adv. in all media.*

"Always write the final draft of your notes as soon as possible after the meeting. That way you will not forget the meaning of your abbreviated words and phrases."

Hector cautioned, "Just remember that formal suggestions like motions or resolutions must be written down word for word. You should even use quotation marks, and write down complete names and figures. For example, if Mr. Smith makes a motion that the company budget $10,000 for advertising in all media and Mrs. Marchi seconds it, you might write down something that looks like this."

Smith — "I move that we budget $10,000 for advertising in all media."
Marchi — "Seconded."

"Remember," warned Hector, "everybody takes notes differently. Write down what you think you will need to remember about what happened at the meeting. Later, you will have to use those notes to write good, complete sentences and paragraphs that other people can read and understand."

"Writing minutes seems like a hard job," said Hector, "but it gets easier the more practice you get. The big secret is to listen carefully and to take accurate notes."

Hector takes thorough minutes at the partners' meetings.

Activity A   On your paper, write the notes you would take from this discussion from a meeting.

Ms. Ives: Because of all the problems we have had with collecting premiums from some of our customers, I move that we hire a collection agency to collect any bill that is over 90 days past due.

Mr. Kingman: Before we vote on that motion, I believe we should look into how much a collection agency will cost us. Also there should be some things the billing department can do before we get outside help.

Mr. Rodrigez: You're right. I think the billing department could make more calls to customers with overdue bills—maybe even send them one or two warning letters.

Ms. Ives: I agree that we should have Ms. Raye, who is in charge of the billing department, come to our next meeting to report on what her department is doing and what more it can do.

Mr. Kingman: Would you put that in the form of motion, please, Ms. Ives?

Ms. Ives: I move that we table my original motion. I also move that we have Ms. Raye report at our next meeting on what the billing department is doing and can do to collect delinquent accounts.

Mr. Rodrigez: I second that motion.

Mr. Kingman: All in favor? Then the motion is carried.

Activity B   On your paper, write minutes for the meeting in Activity A, using the notes you took. (Don't look back at the actual discussion in the textbook.)

Sometimes Smith, Marchi, and Glassman have customers who live out of town or out of the state. As a result, these customers sometimes call long distance or write letters with questions that they need to have answered. Part of Hector and Yuki's job is to answer requests for general information.

For example, a customer who lives in Philadelphia, Pennsylvania, wrote asking if her homeowner's insurance covered the theft of her lawn chairs from her patio. The chairs were missing when she came back from a trip. She wanted to know if her insurance policy included coverage of items that were taken from outside of the house. If so, how much would the insurance company pay and what should she do next?

Hector checked her insurance coverage and wrote her a letter. This is part of the body of that letter.

> You have our standard homeowner's policy. Since your policy has a $100 **deductible** clause, you must pay the first $100 of loss. Then we will pay any loss over $100. If the value of your lawn chairs comes to more than $100, send us the receipt for the cost of the replacements, and we will issue you a check for any amount over $100.

Deductible

A clause in an insurance policy that makes you responsible for paying a certain amount of a loss. For example, if your car is damaged in an accident, you might have to pay the first $100 to have it fixed and the insurance company would pay the rest.

Hector's letter was written well. He stated the kind of policy the customer has and described the coverage. He explained how much the customer will have to pay to replace the lawn chairs and how much the insurance company will pay. He also told the customer exactly what to do.

Activity A Shown below is part of a letter written to a customer who wanted to know how he could increase his life insurance coverage. After you read it, decide what should have been included in the answer but wasn't. Then, on your paper, rewrite the body of the letter to make it better.

According to our records, you presently hold $50,000 worth of life insurance. You can increase that amount of insurance if you wish. I would certainly recommend that you double your present coverage, since you are married and have two small children.

If I can be of any further assistance, please call me.

Hector shows Yuki how to respond to a customer's letter.

Activity B   Number your paper 1 to 4. If a statement is true, write *True* next to the number. If it is not true, write *False*.

1) When responding to letters, give customers all the facts necessary to answer their questions completely.

2) A letter answering a question should be as short as possible.

3) Make customers feel that you take their questions seriously by answering them carefully and completely.

4) Provide every bit of information you can when answering customers' questions.

Activity C   Suppose Mrs. Rose O'Connor has written you a letter asking what kinds of public transportation are available in your city. For example, are there buses or a subway? On a separate sheet of paper, write a letter to Mrs. O'Connor. Give as much information as you can about the public transportation available where you live. Make sure that your letter is clear, easy to understand, accurate, and complete.

Chapter Summary

Making yourself understood is not only an important part of Hector and Yuki's job, but it is also an important part of any job. No matter how you make your living, you should be able to speak and write clearly.

Using the telephone or dealing with customers in person makes it necessary for you to be a good communicator. Your voice should have a pleasant tone, and you should make people feel that you are interested in them and their problems or concerns.

You should treat your coworkers the same way. The telephone messages you take for them should be accurate and easy to read. Minutes you take and letters you write should also be clear and accurate because mistakes can cost your employer or customer money—sometimes a great deal of money. Mistakes and misunderstandings can also waste time and can delay a job from being completed on time.

Since employers want people with good communication skills working for them, remember these nine important points about good communication on the job.

1. Always be polite and helpful.

2. Listen carefully.

3. If you are not sure you understood something, ask for an explanation.

4. If you don't know how to spell a person's name, ask for the correct spelling.

5. Always have a friendly tone to your voice.

6. Make customers feel that you genuinely care about them.

7. Make your writing complete, clear, easy to read, and accurate.

8. Use neat, careful handwriting.

9. If you don't know the answer to a customer's question, take the time to find the answer. If necessary, transfer the customer to someone else who does know the answer.

Part A   Number your paper 1 to 15. If the statement is true, write *True* next to the number. If it is not true, write *False*.

1) An unpleasant voice answering the telephone can make customers take their business elsewhere.

2) When the phone rings, count to ten before you pick up the receiver.

3) If you answer the telephone right away, the customer will think that you are not busy.

4) Always speak with a pleasant voice.

5) Give the name of your company.

6) Don't give your name unless the caller asks for it.

7) Do not ask callers to repeat anything—even if you don't understand them.

8) If customers get nasty first, you can be rude back.

9) Make sure that any messages you take are complete and accurate.

10) End all calls quickly. You don't have time to waste on the telephone.

11) Make customers feel you will do everything you can to help them.

12) Do not mumble.

13) It is all right to use slang as long as you are courteous.

14) You can hang up on customers if they are rude to you.

15) Let customers hang up first. Then you can be sure that they have said everything they want to say.

Part B   On your paper, write the message you would give to your boss as a result of this phone call.

You: H. G. Carbone Company. Mr. Williams speaking.

Caller: Mr. Williams, this is John Denny. I would like to speak to Mr. Carbone.

You: I'm sorry, Mr. Denny, but Mr. Carbone is in a meeting now. May I take a message?

Caller: Yes, tell him to call me as soon as possible at 555-8746. The order he sent me is missing several items, and I want to know why.

Part C   On your paper, take notes on this discussion.

Mr. Rozek: I think that we should hire three new salespeople because our business is growing so fast.

Ms. George: Do our salespeople feel they're overworked? They work on commission; they may not want to give up any of their territories.

Mr. Rozek: I have talked to many of them, and they have many complaints. However, I haven't discussed the possibility of additional staff with them.

Mr. Starbird: I'm not sure the sales staff should make that decision. Are any of our customers complaining about the service they're getting?

Ms. George: I haven't gotten any complaints.

Mr. Starbird: Then I don't see what the problem is.

Mr. Rozek: But what about developing new business? Can our salespeople handle all of their current customers plus have time to get new customers?

Ms. George: I move that Mr. Rozek poll the sales staff to see if they feel that they need help. Afterward, we can decide whether or not we need more salespeople.

Mr. Rozek: I second that motion.

Mr. Starbird: All in favor? The motion is passed.

Part D   On your paper, use the notes you took in Part C to write minutes for that part of the meeting. (Do not look back at the discussion in Part C.)

Part E   Study this situation: You were asked to write a letter to Ms. Carrel Dryer. You are going to ask her to complete a form, which you will enclose in the letter. She is to return it within a week to you. On a piece of paper, write the letter to Ms. Dryer.

Test Taking Tip   When you are reading a test question, look for words such as *mainly, most likely, generally, major,* and *best.* Decide which answer choice fits with the meaning of that word.

Chapter

12

Getting Ahead

Once you have a job in a company, how do you get ahead? In other words, how do you get promoted to a better job? How do you get pay raises? How do you get to become a supervisor?

In Chapter 12, you will find some answers to these questions. This chapter has some good advice for employees who want to go as far as they can in their careers.

Goals for Learning

▶ To understand the benefits of additional education

▶ To become familiar with college forms

▶ To improve your test-taking skills

Nick Pappas was concerned about his career at Henson Mills, where he had worked for eight years. During the first three years, he was promoted several times, but since then he had not received a single promotion. One night he talked with Maria Rivera about his situation. Maria, who also worked for Henson Mills, had been promoted regularly during the ten years she worked there.

"Maria, why don't I get promoted the way you do?" asked Nick.

"One reason is that you haven't bothered to get any additional training," she replied. "You laughed when I told you I went to night school, but the company is changing, and I want to be able to change with it. In fact, my next goal is to learn to program computers."

"What does programming computers have to do with a fabric mill?" Nick asked.

"Plenty," Maria said. "You'd know that if you kept up with what the company is doing. For example, six months from now, the company is installing two looms that will be run by a computer. If they work out, the company plans to get even more. Then what do you think will happen to the people who work the machines now?" Maria asked.

"Wait a minute!" Nick said excitedly. "You mean workers like me are going to be replaced by computers?"

"That's right," Maria replied, "and since the company doesn't have a retraining program, it's up to everyone to get their own training. Those who don't will probably end up without a job."

"What should I do?" Nick asked in a worried voice.

"Well, you could join me and take two computer courses at the community college. The first one is an introduction to computers, and the second one covers beginning programming," Maria suggested. "Then next semester I'm going to take an evening course on advanced programming."

"Well, I'm not too thrilled about giving up my evenings to go back to school," Nick said, "but I'll think about it."

"Don't wait too long. Registration at the community college begins next week," Maria warned.

Nick went home and discussed the idea of additional training with his wife Sara. She thought that his going to school for extra training was a good idea. "You've been upset about not getting ahead in the company. Maybe some extra schooling will help you," she said. "Why don't you ask your boss what he thinks about your going back to school?"

The next day Nick did just what Sara suggested. After he told his boss about the computer courses, his boss said, "Nick, I'm so glad you're thinking about doing something to improve your skills. I was beginning to feel that you didn't want to make the effort needed to do better. Taking those computer courses may be the best decision you'll ever make because this company will need people with that kind of training to serve as supervisors in the future."

The following week Nick and Maria went to the community college to register for the computer courses. There they found lots of other people signing up to take courses. Some, like Nick and Maria, were taking a few courses to improve their job skills or to learn more about a certain subject. Others were taking courses to earn one of several different degrees.

Undergraduate degree

A degree offered for completing a two-year (Associate of Arts) or a four-year (Bachelor of Arts or Bachelor of Science) college program.

You can earn an **undergraduate degree** after completing a two-year or a four-year college program. By completing a college program that contains two years' worth of courses, you can get an associate of arts degree. Another kind of college degree, a bachelor's degree, takes four years of full-time attendance. After earning a bachelor's degree, you can continue your schooling to earn a master's degree and then a doctorate.

After Nick and Maria stood in line for a while, they were given some registration forms to fill out. They were a little confusing to Nick because he didn't understand the meaning of some of these words.

College Form Vocabulary

Course number   A number given to a course to show that it is different from all the other courses. Course numbers are found in college catalogs and course listings.

Course title   The name of the course; for example, *Computers for the Beginner* or *Computers 101.*

Course description   An explanation of what is taught in the course. This information is usually found in a college catalog.

Degree desired   The degree program that a student is working to complete, such as A. A. (Associate of Arts), B. A. (Bachelor of Arts), or B. S. (Bachelor of Science).

Section   One of several class offerings of the same course.

Credit   Points given by a college to a student who has successfully finished a course. Most college courses take half of a school year to complete.

Registration form

A form used to sign up for college courses.

Following is an example of the **registration form** that Nick and Maria had to fill out in order to take the college courses.

Strasburgh College
Registration Form

(Please print or type)

Name ___ *Pappas* _____ *Nick* _____ *F.* ___
             Last   First   Middle Initial

Address ___ *10 Elm Street* _____

___ *Miami,* _____ *FL* _____ *33153* ___
         City   State   ZIP

Course No.	Section	Title	Days Offered	Credits
736 - 1000	3	Computer I	Tu	3
736 - 1004	1	Programming I	W	3

___ *Nick F. Pappas* ___
Signature

Nick printed his name and address according to the instructions on the form. He looked into the college catalog to get the correct course number and title. Then he copied the section number, days offered, and credits from a course listing that he had been given when he arrived.

Nick filled out the form very carefully because he wanted to make sure that he got into the right classes. He asked Maria to check his form—just to make doubly sure he had filled everything out correctly.

Activity A Number your paper 1 to 7. Then match each word in the first column with its meaning in the second column.

Vocabulary Word

1) course description
2) days offered
3) section
4) course number
5) credit
6) course title
7) degree desired

Meaning

a) number assigned to a course to tell it apart from other courses
b) the day or days of the week when a course is taught
c) the program taken to earn an associate or bachelor's degree
d) the name of the course
e) an explanation of the content of a course
f) the particular section of a course
g) the number of points earned for a course

Lesson 2   Other Forms

College application

A form used to request admission to college as a degree candidate.

Degree candidate

Someone seeking to complete a degree program and earn a college diploma.

Nick's friend, Peg O'Reilly, was also taking college courses. However, Peg was planning to get her degree from Central College. In addition to the forms that Nick and Maria had to fill out, she also had to complete a **college application** for admission to college as a **degree candidate**. When Peg showed the five-page form to Nick, he laughed and said, "Filling out all that information would take me all night!"

"No, it wouldn't," smiled Peg. "It's not hard to complete these forms once you understand what information they're asking for."

On page 205 is the first page of Peg's application form.

Application for CENTRAL COLLEGE

(Miss)
Mrs.

1. Name in full: Mr. _O'Reilly_   _Peggy_   _Nora_   2.   Sex _F_
                        Last   First   Middle

3. Permanent home address _211 5th Street_   _Miami_   _Dade_   _FL_   _33152_
                           Number/Route Street   City   County   State   ZIP

   Mailing address (if different from #3) _N/A_
                           Number/Route Street   City   County   State   ZIP

4. Soc. Sec. No. _318-58-0745_   Phone No. _407 555-3122_   Emergency Phone No. _407 555-4873_

5. (a) Date of birth ___2 / 12 / 70___   Age _31_   (b) Place of birth _Ocala, FL_
                      Month / Day / Year

   (c) If not born in the United States, when and where were you naturalized? _N/A_

6. Married Yes _____   No _✓_

7. Name and   Father _Samuel O'Reilly, Ocala, FL 32670_   Phone No. _586-1621_
   address of   Mother _Elaine O'Reilly, Same_   Phone No. _Same_
                Guardian _____   Phone No. _____

8. (a) List all senior high schools attended:

Name of School	Location	Years of Attendance	Date of Graduation
Ocala Senior High	Ocala, FL	1984 - 1988	1988

   (b) Have you received a GED?   Yes____ No _✓_ Date you received your GED:_____
   (I have taken)/ I plan to take the Scholastic Aptitude Test (Date) _7/6/01_ and will have
   the results forwarded.

9. (a) List all colleges and/or universities attended:

Name	City & State	Dates Attended	Reasons for Leaving	# of Credits Completed
N/A				

   (b) If ever suspended or dismissed, please explain in detail on separate attached sheet.
   (c) Have you ever attended Central College? No _✓_ Full____ Part-Time ___ Evening ___
       Summer _____   Last Date _____

10. (a) In what extracurricular activities have you participated in high school? For example,
        athletics, dramatics, music, publications, etc. List offices held. List in order of preference.
        1. _Newspaper (editor)_   2. _Yearbook_
        3. _Glee Club_   4. _____

    (b) Name any special honors you have received in school _Honor Roll_

11. Work experiences, including summer or part-time employment. If you are not a recent high
    school graduate, you must account for each year intervening between date of leaving high
    school and date of this application. (Use separate sheet if necessary.)

Type of Work	Name and Address of Employer	Phone Number	Dates of Employment	Part- or Full-Time	Salary
Administrative	S. Franz, 2387 Flagler St.	407 555-1175	1988 to	Full-	$19370
Assistant	Miami, FL 33154		Present	time	per year

Activity A Number your paper 1 to 10. Then match the item from Peg's application form in the first column with the information you would need to complete that item in the second column. Peg's application is shown on page 205.

Application Item

1) emergency phone number

2) place of birth

3) married

4) list colleges attended

5) extracurricular activities

6) work experiences

7) type of work

8) dates of employment

9) salary

10) years of attendance

Information Needed

a) date when you began to work for a company and date when you stopped working for that company

b) a number the college can call to inform someone if you are sick or hurt

c) the city and state where you were born

d) a list of the jobs you have held up to this time

e) married? (answer *yes* or *no*)

f) clubs or organizations you joined in school and which were not part of the regular school program

g) the kind of work that you did for a company

h) the amount you were paid

i) the year you started in a school and the year you left that school

j) the names of colleges you attended

Rolf Muller, another friend of Nick's, was taking an **adult education** course at the night school in a local high school. There are several reasons why people attend night school. One reason is to take a course to get a special skill, such as keyboarding or woodworking. Another is to learn more about a certain subject such as a foreign language. A third reason is to earn a high school diploma.

That's what Rolf wanted to do. Because he had not graduated from high school when he should have, he decided to finish at night. Rolf asked Nick for some help in filling out the application form for night school.

To earn a high school diploma, Rolf would have to take and pass a test. The test covers the material taught in the major courses offered in high school. Nick helped Rolf choose some courses that would help Rolf pass the test.

Nick and Maria learned new skills in their computer class at the community college.

**Grand City Public Schools — Adult Education Division
Night-School Application**

(Please print or type.)

Muller	Rolf	T.
Name (Last)	(First)	(Initial)

27 Lynch Circle   33162
Address   (ZIP Code)

407 555-1112   407 555-2899
Telephone Number   Emergency Telephone

Flagler High School, 1700 Rise Drive
Name and Address of Last School Attended

10th   1982
Highest Grade Completed   Last Year Attended

How did you find out about this night-school center?
A neighbor told me.

What are your educational goals?
I would like to get my high school diploma.

List below the course or courses you wish to take.
English III   Algebra I

Activity B   Number your paper 1 to 12. Then answer these questions about the application form above.

1) Why do you think the instructions tell you to print or type?

2) What is Mr. Muller's first name and middle initial?

3) What is his ZIP code?

4) If Mr. Muller got sick at school or had an accident, what number could the people in the school call?

5) Where did Mr. Muller go to high school?

6) When did he leave high school?

7) Did he graduate from high school? How can you tell?

8) How did Mr. Muller find out about this night school?

9) What two courses does Mr. Muller want to take now?

10) Is this the only time Mr. Muller will attend night school? How do you know?

11) Many night schools have guidance counselors who work with students to make sure that they get into the best program. Why do you think the counselor would be especially interested in a student's educational goals?

12) Why do you think the application asks for the name and address of the last school attended?

After a few weeks of their course, Nick and Maria's teacher announced that there would be a test the following week. "I've been dreading that," moaned Nick. "It's been years since I took a test, and as I recall, I never did very well on tests. Sometimes I get so nervous that I can't even think straight."

"Have you understood everything we've learned so far in class?" asked Maria.

"Yes, in fact, I feel very good about the material because I have studied between classes, read all the chapters the teacher assigned, and done all the homework," Nick said. Then he added, "It's just that tests make me so nervous."

"They used to bother me too, but a while ago a teacher taught me some techniques for taking tests. I haven't had any trouble since," Maria explained.

"Please tell me what those techniques are," Nick pleaded with Maria. "They sound like what I need to make a good grade!"

These are the techniques that Maria explained to Nick.

1. **Thoroughly know the material the test will cover.**

   Do not wait until just before a test to study. Study each new piece of material as it is given to you. Keep up with reading assignments. Take careful notes as you read. Review your notes regularly. If some information is not clear to you, ask questions until you understand it completely.

2. **Budget the time that you have to take the test.**

   Before you begin a test, skim over it. Get an idea of the number and type of questions on the test. Then figure out how much time you have for the whole test and how much time you can spend on each question. True/false and multiple-choice questions usually require the least amount of time. Questions that require a two- or three-sentence response need more time, and questions that require an essay for an answer need the most time. If, for example, you have an hour to finish a test, try to be halfway through in 30 minutes. Pace yourself. Then, if you finish the test early, take the leftover time to look over your answers.

3. **Read each question carefully.**

   Answer the questions that are asked, not the questions you hoped would be asked. If you don't read a question correctly, you will end up giving a wrong answer. For example, suppose one question asked, "Where is the input button?" If you read the question quickly, you might think it asked, "When is the input button used?" It is easy to see why your answer would be wrong.

4. **Save any questions you are not sure of for last.**

   If you are not sure of an answer, continue through to the end of the test. After you have finished, answer any questions that you skipped earlier. If this is the kind of test that has no penalty for unanswered questions, answer only those questions that you are reasonably sure of.

5. **Concentrate on the parts of the test that are worth the most points.**

   If you have been told that some parts of the test are worth more points than others, concentrate on the parts that are worth the most points.

6. **Mark your answers clearly and accurately.**

   Preprinted answer sheet

   A form on which students mark answers to tests by filling in circles, circling letters, etc.

   Preprinted answer sheets are often scored by computer. Check the numbering of your answer sheet often as you write your answers on it. Also make sure your marks are dark. If you skip a question, also skip a space on the answer sheet. Finally, be sure you know what to do if you want to change an answer.

7. **Change answers only if you have a good reason for doing so.**

   Usually it's best not to change an answer based on a hunch or a whim. However, if you believe you have good evidence that your first answer may be wrong, change your answer.

Activity A   Number your paper 1 to 16. If the statement is true, write *True* next to the number. If it is not true, write *False*.

1) You will do better on a test if you wait to study the night before the test.

2) Study each new piece of material as it is given.

3) Do your reading assignments all at one time.

4) Don't ask questions in class because asking questions will make the teacher think you didn't read the assignment.

5) If you read a question on a test incorrectly, your answer probably will also be wrong.

6) Before you begin to take a test, look it over to see how many and what kinds of questions you will have to answer.

7) If you are not sure of the answer to some questions, skip them and go on to finish the test. Then go back to those questions.

8) Allow the most time for multiple-choice questions and the least time for questions that require an essay.

9) If you have been told how much each part of a test is worth, concentrate on those parts that are worth the most points.

10) If you are using a preprinted answer sheet, check the numbering of your answers often.

11) If you are taking a test that doesn't take off points for unanswered questions, guess as many answers as you can.

12) When you do your reading assignments, take good notes.

13) If you have a hunch that the answer you gave on a test is wrong, change it before you turn in your test.

14) Change an answer only if you are very sure that you are changing it to the correct answer.

15) Never skip a question.

16) If you finish a test early, look over your answers.

Activity B   Number your paper 1 to 4. Then write answers to these questions.

1) Your test has 20 multiple-choice questions. You have 50 minutes to take the test. About how long should you allow for each question?

2) The true/false section of a test is worth 25 points. The essay section is worth 45 points. The short-answer section is worth 30 points. On which section should you spend the most time?

3) You have three hours to take a test. It has three parts. The first part has 25 multiple-choice questions. The reading part of each question is fairly long. This part of the test is worth 35 points. The second part of the test has 10 questions that require 2- to 3-sentence answers. This section is worth 20 points. The last part of the test has two essay questions. Each question requires an answer that is several paragraphs long. This section is worth 45 points. How will you budget the three hours you have to take this test?

4) You have been given a standardized test that contains 100 multiple-choice questions. You have three hours to take this test. You should
- answer as many questions as possible.
- allow time to check the numbering of your preprinted answer sheet.
- go back and answer any questions that you skipped.
- reread any answers you weren't sure about.

How would you budget the three hours you have for this test?

Nick applied his test-taking skills to pass his final exam.

Sometimes the jobs that people are hired to do change because of new technology and new ideas. In fact, it is very likely that during the years you work, you will need to be trained to do something different—to use a new piece of equipment or to use a new procedure. Often this training will include taking courses in colleges, universities, or other adult education centers. When you register for these kinds of training programs, you will need to fill out some forms. These completed forms must be correct and neat if you want to be sure to get into the right program.

When you take courses, you will also have to take tests. The following suggestions will help you improve your test-taking skills: (1) study the course material as it is given, (2) take careful notes, (3) budget the time you have to take a test, (4) read test questions carefully, (5) spend the most time on the parts of a test that are worth the most points, (6) mark your answers carefully when you use a preprinted answer sheet, and (7) change an answer only if you have a good reason to do so.

Part A Number your paper 1 to 5. Then write the correct answer in the box to complete each sentence. (Use each answer only once.)

number	days offered	section
title	degree desired	
credits	descriptions	

1) A college catalog has course _____ that explain what will be taught in each class.

2) To identify a particular class in a catalog, look for three things: the course _____ , the course _____ , and the _____ .

3) You must also know the _____ _____ for each class in order to get to a particular class at the right time.

4) A college gives _____ for each course taken. They can be used toward getting a diploma.

5) If you want a diploma, you should indicate the _____ _____ on your application to take courses.

Part B Number your paper 1 to 20. Then write the information that you would place on the lines of a college application containing each of these terms.

1) emergency phone no.

2) date of birth

3) place of birth

4) name of father

5) high school attended

6) years attended

7) date of graduation

8) special honors

9) colleges attended

10) extracurricular activities

11) work experiences

12) dates of employment

13) salary of each job

14) age

15) sex

16) Social Security number

17) your ZIP code

18) name of mother

19) community activities

20) mailing address if different

Part C   Number your paper 1 to 10. Then write the word needed to complete each of these sentences about taking a test.

1) Make sure that you _____ the directions for a test.

2) If you don't, _____ the teacher to explain the directions.

3) Read the questions _____ .

4) Before you _____ a test, look it over.

5) Also notice the _____ of questions.

6) Figure out how much time you have for the _____ test.

7) Figure out how much time you can devote to each _____ .

8) Allow the _____ time for true/false questions.

9) Allow the _____ time for essay questions.

10) Spend the most time on the parts of the test that are _____ the most points.

Test Taking Tip   When you are taking a multiple-choice test, read every choice before you answer a question. Put a line through choices you know are wrong. Then choose the best answer from the remaining choices.

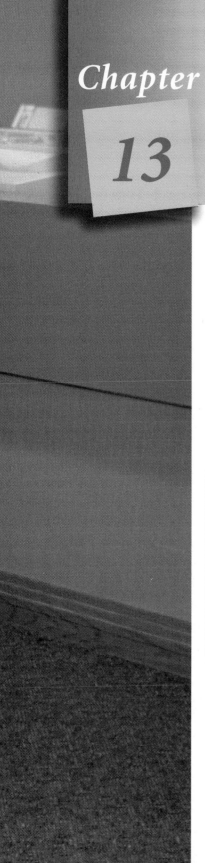

Chapter 13

Medical Coverage for Employees

One of the advantages of full-time employment can be the ability to get health insurance at a lower, group rate. To receive any kind of health benefits, you will have to fill out some forms. However, the time and work the forms will take to complete certainly will be worthwhile if you or any of your dependents ever need medical care.

In Chapter 13, you will learn how to accurately and completely fill out the various forms needed to get medical benefits. Each lesson will cover a different kind of form.

Goals for Learning

▶ To understand the value of health insurance

▶ To be able to fill out a health insurance form correctly

▶ To learn the procedure for applying for health benefits

▶ To understand the process involved in workers' compensation

▶ To be able to fill out an accident report completely

Group insurance
Insurance bought by a large group of people, such as employees of a company.

Human resources
The part of the company that deals with employees. Another name for this department is personnel.

Medical insurance
An agreement in which a person pays a given amount to an insurance company so that the insurance company will pay certain medical bills.

Premium
The amount of money paid to an insurance company for insurance protection.

When Nithia Rao began working for Ted E. Baer, Inc., she applied for **medical insurance**, which helps people pay bills caused by illness, injury, or accident. The **premium**, or payment, for that insurance protection was subtracted from her weekly paycheck. However, by getting the insurance through her job, the rates were much lower than if she had to buy the insurance on her own. Medical insurance is less expensive when a large group of people buy it together as **group insurance**. Some companies also offer life insurance in a group plan.

For the next three years, Nithia paid the premiums, but she never had to use her health insurance. Then she learned she needed an operation that would involve a two-day stay in the hospital. Because she had insurance, Nithia didn't have to pay anything to the hospital or to her doctor. Her insurance covered all medical expenses.

To apply for her insurance, Nithia went to the personnel, or **human resources**, office at her company. There, one of the counselors gave her an application to fill out and later helped her check the application to make sure it was correct.

This is the form that Nithia filled out.

Medical Insurance Application

Name: Rao (Last)   Nithia (First)   M. (Middle)

Employer: Ted E. Baer, Inc.

Home Address (include ZIP Code): 1223 Long Blvd. Atlanta, GA 98716

Date of Birth: 3/12/72

Spouse's Date of Birth: 7/21/72

_____ Male
✓ Female
0 No. of dependents

_____ Single
✓ Married
_____ Widowed
_____ Divorced

No Does your spouse have group health insurance with another employer, union, etc.?

Signature: *Nithia M. Rao*

Date: 3/18/01

Nithia followed all the directions, giving her birth date and the birth date of her husband. She also put a zero beside *No. of dependents* because she didn't have children or anyone else who depended on her for food, shelter, and clothing.

If Nithia had not filled the form out correctly, her husband might not have been covered under her policy. Because he was not covered by any other health plan, he really needed to be covered under her policy.

Nithia had to pay additional money to have her husband covered under her policy. The premium, however, was still much lower than if her husband bought insurance on his own. Being covered under a group insurance plan really helped Nithia and her husband. They had medical coverage for a price they could afford. They did not have to worry about medical care.

Activity A Number your paper 1 to 11. Then write the information you would put on each line if you were filling out this application for health insurance for yourself.

Medical Insurance Application

(1)
Name   (Last)   (First)   (Middle)   **(2)** Employer

(3)
Home Address (include ZIP Code)

(4)   **(5)**
Date of Birth   Spouse's Date of Birth

(6)___ Male   **(7)** ___ Single   **(8)**___ Does your spouse have
___ Female   ___ Married   group health insurance
(9)___ No. of   ___ Widowed   with another employer,
        dependents   ___ Divorced   union, ect.?

Signature _____ **(10)** _____ Date ___ **(11)** _____

Before Nithia went to the hospital for her operation, she had to complete another form. This form guaranteed that her health insurance company would directly pay the doctor and hospital bills. Some health insurance companies send their payments directly to the patient, who then pays the hospital and doctor. However, Nithia's insurance didn't work that way. She had to complete a form before she went into the hospital in order to get her insurance company to pay her doctor directly. Once she had filled out her part of the form, she took it to her doctor's office so that the doctor's secretary could fill out the rest of the form and send it to the insurance company.

To make sure that she filled out her portion of the form correctly, she called the insurance company to get an explanation of some of the terms on the form. The call didn't even cost her anything because she found a **toll-free**, 800 number on the application.

Toll-free
Without cost.

1. The **patient** is the person who is being treated. In Nithia's case, she wrote her own name. If her husband were the one having the operation, she would have written his name on the form.

Patient
A person being treated for a medical problem.

2. The employee or **insuree** is the employed person who has the insurance. Nithia wrote her own name. Even if her husband were being treated, Nithia would write her name here because the insurance is in her name. Some forms use the term *insuree's name*, which means the same as *employee's name*.

Insuree
A person who has insurance coverage.

3. *Do you have other health insurance coverage?*—This question asks if you have any other medical insurance. If you do, you are supposed to write down the name of the other insurance company. In Nithia's case, she wrote *No*. It's important that you complete this item carefully because if you say you have other coverage and you don't, your health insurance company may not pay all the benefits that you're entitled to.

4. *Was the condition related to the patient's employment?*—This question asks if the medical illness or injury had anything to do with the patient's job. In Nithia's case, she wrote *No* because her medical problem was not caused by her job. This answer also affects the amount of medical benefits the insurance company will pay.

Nithia was smart because she called her insurance company for an explanation of some insurance terms that she wasn't familiar with. As a result, she was confident that she had filled out the form correctly.

Activity A Number your paper 1 to 4. Then fill in the words that complete the definitions of the four terms that Nithia asked her insurance company to explain.

1) patient's name

the name of the _____ who is being _____

2) employee's name

the name of the _____ who carries the _____

3) Do you have other insurance coverage?

the name of any other _____ with which you

have _____

4) Was the condition related to the patient's employment?

Did your _____ have anything to do with

your _____ ?

Reading a Health-Benefit Form

On page 222 is a sample of the health-benefit form that Nithia completed so that the insurance company would pay her doctor's and hospital's bills. Notice that she was supposed to fill out only the top part of the form. The doctor or the person or company supplying the medical service was supposed to complete the rest of the form.

MAJOR MEDICAL CLAIM

PATIENT & EMPLOYEE INFORMATION

1 PATIENT'S NAME *(First name, middle initial, last name)*	2 PATIENT'S DATE OF BIRTH	3 EMPLOYEE'S NAME *(First name, middle initial, last name)*

4 PATIENT'S ADDRESS *(Street, city, state, ZIP code)*	5 PATIENT'S SEX MALE ☐ FEMALE ☐	6 EMPLOYEE'S DATE OF BIRTH
	7 PATIENT'S RELATIONSHIP TO EMPLOYEE SELF SPOUSE CHILD OTHER	8 EMPLOYEE'S GROUP NO. *(Or group name)*

9 OTHER HEALTH INSURANCE COVERAGE - Enter Name of Policyholder and Plan Name and Address and Policy or Medical Assistance Number	10 WAS CONDITION RELATED TO A PATIENT'S EMPLOYMENT YES ☐ NO B AN AUTO ACCIDENT YES ☐ NO	11 EMPLOYEE'S ADDRESS *(Street, city, state, ZIP code)*

12 PATIENT'S OR AUTHORIZED PERSON'S SIGNATURE I Authorize the Release of any Medical Information Necessary to Process this Claim and Request Payment of MEDICARE/CHAMPUS Benefits either to Myself or to the Party Who Accepts Assignment Below. SIGNED DATE	13 I AUTHORIZE PAYMENT OF MEDICAL BENEFITS TO UNDERSIGNED PHYSICIAN OR SUPPLIER FOR SERVICE DESCRIBED BELOW SIGNED *(Employee or Authorized Person)*

PHYSICIAN OR SUPPLIER INFORMATION

14 DATE OF	ILLNESS (FIRST SYMPTOM) OR INJURY (ACCIDENT) OR PREGNANCY (LMP)	15 DATE FIRST CONSULTED YOU FOR THIS CONDITION	16 HAS PATIENT EVER HAD SAME OR SIMILAR SYMPTOMS? YES ☐ NO
17 DATE PATIENT ABLE TO RETURN TO WORK	18 DATES OF TOTAL DISABILITY FROM THROUGH		DATES OF PARTIAL DISABILITY FROM THROUGH
19 NAME OF REFERRING PHYSICIAN			20 FOR SERVICE RELATED TO HOSPITALIZATION GIVE HOSPITALIZATION DATES ADMITTED DISCHARGED
21 NAME & ADDRESS OF FACILITY WHERE SERVICES RENDERED *(If other than home or office)*			22 WAS LABORATORY WORK PERFORMED OUTSIDE YOUR OFFICE? YES ☐ NO CHARGES

23 DIAGNOSIS OR NATURE OF ILLNESS OR INJURY. RELATE DIAGNOSIS TO PROCEDURE IN COLUMN D BY REFERENCE TO NUMBERS 1,2,3, ECT. OR DX CODE

1

2

3

4

24 A DATE OF SERVICE	B * PLACE OF SERV-ICE	C PROCEDURE CODE (IDENTIFY)	FULLY DESCRIBE PROCEDURES, MEDICAL SERVICES OR SUPPLIES FURNISHED FOR EACH DATE GIVEN *(EXPLAIN UNUSUAL SERVICES OR CIRCUMSTANCES)*	D DIAGNOSIS CODE	E CHARGES	F

25 SIGNATURE OF PHYSICIAN OR SUPPLIER	26 ACCEPT ASSIGNMENT (GOVERNMENT CLAIMS ONLY) YES ☐ NO	27 TOTAL CHARGE	28 AMOUNT PAID	29 BALANCE DUE
	30 YOUR SOCIAL SECURITY NO.	31 PHYSICIAN'S OR SUPPLIER'S NAME, ADDRESS, ZIP CODE & TELEPHONE NO.		
SIGNED DATE				
32 YOUR PATIENT'S ACCOUNT NO	33 YOUR EMPLOYER I.D. NO.			
	I.D. NO.			

* PLACE OF SERVICE CODES
  1 - (IH) - INPATIENT HOSPITAL
  2 - (OH) - OUTPATIENT HOSPITAL
  3 - (O)   - DOCTOR'S OFFICE
  4 - (H)   - PATIENT'S HOME
  5 -   - DAY CARE FACILITY (PSY)
  6 -   - NIGHT CARE FACILITY (PSY)

  7 - (NH) - NURSING HOME
  8 - (SNF)- SKILLED NURSING FACILITY
  9 -   - AMBULANCE
  0 - (OL) - OTHER LOCATIONS
  A - (IL) - INDEPENDENT LABORATORY
  B -   - OTHER MEDICAL/ SURGICAL FACILITY

Activity B Number your paper 1 to 7. Then write short answers to these questions about the health-benefits form on page 222.

1) Suppose your mother lives with you and is dependent on you. If she is the person receiving medical treatment, where would you write her name, address, date of birth, sex, and her relationship to you?

2) If your mother is the patient, do you put your name anywhere on this form? If so, where?

3) If your mother is the patient, what other information would you still have to include about yourself?

4) If you were the patient, in what two places would you write your name?

5) Who must sign this form?

6) Who fills out most of the information on this form?

7) Why do you think that the doctor has to supply so much information?

Lesson 3   **Workers' Compensation**

Workers' compensation

Benefits paid to employees who are injured or disabled on the job.

If Nithia had an accident on the job or if her medical problem was job related, she could have applied for a different kind of insurance called **workers' compensation**. Employers are required by law to have this kind of insurance so that they can help their employees who have job-related accidents or illnesses pay their medical bills. In some states, employees who have to miss work because of job-related injuries also receive a part of their paychecks.

After workers apply for workers' compensation, a board studies their applications and medical records and then decides whether or not they are entitled to get these benefits. On page 224 is an application form for workers' compensation that was completed by Mike Jupo, Nithia's friend who works at the Oregon branch of Ted E. Baer, Inc. Notice that this application has several lines for a description of how the accident occurred.

State Worker's Compensation Board

(Type or print.)

Jupo	Michael	J		718 - 32 - 0735
Name (Last)	(First)	(Middle)		Soc. Sec. No.

766 Strand	Salem	OR	97302
Address	City	State	ZIP

M	27	Mechanic
Sex	Age	Occupation

Ted E. Baer, Inc. 1550 Desalle Salem, OR 97302
Employer's Name and Address

$450.00	11 / 17 / 01
Wages per Week	Date of Injury

How did the accident occur?
While I was changing a tire on a company truck, the jack slipped. My hand was hit by the bumper as the truck fell.

What kind of injury did you receive? I broke four fingers.

Have you been treated by a doctor for this injury? Yes

Dr. M. Santos 1417 Long Street Salem, OR 97302
Name and Address of Doctor

Signature Michael J. Jupo Date 11 / 20 / 01

Activity A Number your paper 1 to 15. Then write short answers to these questions about the workers' compensation application shown above.

1) What is the full name of the person applying for workers' compensation?

2) How old is Mike?

3) Where does Mike live?

4) How much does Mike earn each week?

5) When did the accident happen?

6) How was Mike injured? (Use your own words.)

7) What kind of injury did Mike have?

8) Did Mike have a doctor look at his injury?

9) What is this doctor's name?

10) Where is this doctor's office?

11) Did Mike make any mistakes in filling out this form?

12) Why do you think the workers' compensation board has to know how much Mike earns?

13) Why do you think the board has to know how the accident happened and who Mike's doctor is?

14) If Mike can't work for one month, how much will he lose? If Mike can't work for two months, how much will he lose?

15) What is the name of the company Mike works for?

Lesson 4   Accident Reports

Accident report

A form that must be completed when an employee is injured on the job.

Nearly all businesses insist that an employee who is injured on the job fill out an **accident report**. Many of these accident reports are similar to the application for workers' compensation. Still, Mike did not understand some of the terms that he needed to know in order to complete the company's accident-report form.

Mike thought he understood the meanings of shift, **safety equipment,** and supervisor, but he was confused by the way the words were used on the form. He wanted to use the word **witnesses** in his description of the accident, but he wasn't sure of the correct spelling. Someone in the personnel office helped him complete the form correctly.

Safety equipment

Protective gear such as goggles or a hard hat that is required for protection on some jobs.

Activity A   Number your paper 1 to 4. Then match each term in the first column with its definition or example in the second column.

Witnesses

The people who saw the accident and could tell what happened.

Term	Meaning
1) safety equipment	**a)** 7:00 A.M.–3:00 P.M., 3:00 P.M.–11:00 P.M., and 11:00 P.M.–7:00 A.M.
2) supervisor	
3) witnesses	
4) shifts	**b)** people who saw what happened
	c) your direct boss
	d) heavy work gloves

Activity B On your paper, list the numbers of five items on this accident report that contain mistakes. Then briefly describe each mistake.

Accident Report Form

1. Date this report ___9/13/01___
2. Date incident occurred

MONTH/DAY/YEAR	TIME	SHIFT	SUPERVISOR
9/13/01	9:10 a.m.	8:30 a.m. - 4:30 p.m.	M. Lee

3. Social Security No. ___356-00-7611___
4. Employee's name (Last, First, Middle Init.) ___Race, Franklin R.___
5. Job title ___Plumber___
6. Home address ___1971 Fine Ave.___
7. Phone   H ___(309) 555-1111___   W ___(309) 555-0723___
8. Date of Birth ___2/12/60___
9. Age ___41___
10. Sex ☑ male ☐ female
11. Date of employment _____
    Date assigned to present job ___6/90___
12. Gross rate of pay ___$9.50___ per ___hour___ (hour, day, week)
13. Specify exact address where incident occurred.
    Also specify exact location at this address.
    ___1000 Blair Road___

14. Describe fully how incident occurred. (Use additional signed sheets if necessary.)
    ___The thing blew up.___
    ___Witnesses saw smoke coming from the machine.___

15. Was safety equipment provided?   ☑ yes   ☐ no
    Was it in use at the time?   ☑ yes   ☐ no
16. According to employee, what part(s) of his/her body were injured?
    _____
17. Employee's signature ___Franklin Race___ ☐ check here if unable to sign

When you begin a new job, always ask if the company offers any health insurance. If it does, you will have to go to the personnel office, or human resources office, to fill out an application to get the insurance and any other benefits.

Then if you become sick, you and your doctor have to fill out another form to guarantee that the insurance company will pay your doctor or hospital bills. Some companies may pay you, and then you will have to pay the doctor or hospital bills. Mistakes on these forms can cost you money and time.

Nithia found out how helpful insurance benefits were. Because she had applied for and paid for medical insurance, all of her medical bills were paid when she had to go into the hospital. If she didn't have the insurance, she might have had to do without the operation.

If you are hurt on the job, you may also be eligible to apply for workers' compensation. To receive these benefits, you will have to fill out an application form. The completed form is passed on to a workers' compensation board that will either accept or deny your request. If you do not fill out your form correctly, the board may deny your request or delay your payment.

No one plans to be injured on the job. If it happens, using proper procedures and correctly filling out the necessary forms, such as accident report forms, make things easier for everyone.

When you fill out any of the forms discussed in this chapter, make sure that you fill in all the information, that you give complete and correct answers, and that you write clearly. If you don't understand some of the terms on any of the forms, ask for some help either from your company's personnel office or from the insurance company itself.

Part A   Number your paper 1 to 10. If the statement is true, write *True* next to the number. If the statement is not true, write *False*.

1) If you don't fill a medical form out correctly, you can always fill out another one later when you have an emergency.

2) Applications for workers' compensation may be either approved or rejected by a special board of people.

3) Group insurance is usually less expensive than individual insurance.

4) A premium is the money the insurance company pays you if you are sick or injured.

5) All insurance companies pay the doctors' and hospitals' bills directly.

6) Health insurance applications usually ask if you are married and have any dependents.

7) When filling out an insurance form, the name of the patient and the insuree are always the same.

8) If you are hurt on the job, you don't have to do anything. You will get workers' compensation automatically.

9) On an application for health insurance, you should never tell that you are insured by another insurance company.

10) You probably will have to fill out an accident report if you get injured on the job.

Part B   Number your paper 1 to 5. Then write short answers to these questions about an application for health insurance benefits.

1) If an application for health insurance benefits asks for the *patient's name*, what information do you put in that blank?

2) In what space on the application would you put the name of the person who has the insurance?

3) What information would you put in a blank on the application that says, *Other health insurance coverage?*

4) What information would you put in a blank on the application that says, *Was condition related to the patient's employment?*

5) Why does the insurance company need to know the patient's name and the insuree's name?

Part C   Number your paper 1 to 5. Then write short answers to these questions that refer to the application for workers' compensation on page 224.

1) Does the application ask for the Social Security number of the person applying for benefits?

2) Why would the workers' compensation board need to know the name and the address of the company for which this person worked?

3) What information does the application ask the person to supply about the accident? (List five items.)

4) Why do you think this application asks the person to give a full description of how the accident happened?

5) Why is it important for the workers' compensation board to know the name and address of the doctor or hospital who treated the person?

Test Taking Tip   If you must decide if a statement is true or false, look for key words such as all, none, always, and never.

Chapter 14

Writing Business Reports

S ome jobs will require that you be able to write a business report or to present one orally. Although much of what you have learned about writing reports in school will apply to writing a business report, there are a few new things that you will have to know.

In Chapter 14, you will learn the six steps for writing a business report. You will also learn how to effectively present a report orally.

Goals for Learning

▶ To determine the purpose of a business report and to create an action plan for one

▶ To collect information from various sources and arrange the information in a logical order for a business report

▶ To make an outline of a business report

▶ To know how to write conclusions and recommendations

▶ To write a business report and be able to present it orally

Julia Michaels had worked for Linsey-Wolsey Company for six years. She was a good employee and had been promoted several times. Then one day her boss, Mrs. Kowalski, took her aside and said, "Julia, I would like to recommend you for the vacancy that will be coming up in the sales department when Mr. Huyhen retires. However, to qualify for the job, you would have to learn some new skills."

"What kinds of skills?" Julia asked.

Business report

A written presentation of information about a business situation.

Mrs. Kowalski explained, "For this job, you will have to learn how to speak in front of groups of people. You will need to know how to give oral and written **business reports**. The position also provides the opportunity to travel to other parts of the state and other parts of the country. The company is worried about finding the right person to replace Mr. Huyhen. I think you could be the right person. In order to be considered for the position, however, you will have to learn a lot very quickly."

Then she added, "Julia, you have an opportunity to turn your job into a career. If you get this promotion, you can move up in this company. This promotion could be very important to you."

Conclusions

Final, logical judgments based on facts.

Julia was so determined to get this promotion that she asked Mr. Huyhen to help her learn what she needed to know to be successful in the new position. When he agreed, they decided to meet a half an hour before work every day.

Recommendations

Suggestions based on information gathered and conclusions reached.

The first thing that Mr. Huyhen helped Julia with was how to write a business report, a written record that presents investigated facts about a business situation and that offers **conclusions** and **recommendations** based on those facts.

He explained that most business people write reports so that they can share information they have with others. Julia needed to learn the kind of information that should be included in a business report. She also needed to know how to put the information together in a clear way. To help her, Mr. Huyhen wrote all the steps for writing a business report on a piece of paper and gave it to Julia. He explained that the steps in writing a business report are not always done in exactly the same order.

Action plan

Steps needed to complete a business report.

Outline

A summary of written work.

Logical order

The arrangement of information in a way that will make sense to a reader.

Steps for Writing a Business Report

1. Write answers to the following questions:

   - Why am I writing this report?

   - What is its purpose?

   - What questions should this report answer?

2. Make an **action plan** for completing the report. Set dates when each part of the plan should be completed. Develop a brief **outline** of the report.

3. Collect the information you need to answer your questions.

4. Make a final outline that arranges your information in a **logical order**.

5. Plan how you will explain or summarize any information your readers may not understand. At the end, draw conclusions from your information and make recommendations if needed.

6. Then follow these steps:

   - Write a rough draft of your report.

   - Proofread it carefully.

   - Make any necessary changes and corrections.

   - Be sure that the final copy of your report is free of errors.

Finding the Purpose

Julia and Mr. Huyhen decided to discuss each of these six steps separately. They started by looking at how to decide the purpose of a report. Mr. Huyhen told Julia to always consider these four questions.

Questions to Determine Purpose

1. WHY is this report being written?
2. For WHOM is this report being written?
3. HOW will this report be used?
4. HOW MUCH should this report cover?

Mr. Huyhen explained, "Suppose at a sales meeting you mention that customers are complaining about one of our products. It's likely that Ms. Ohara, the supervisor, would ask you to write a report about what you and the other salespeople are hearing about this product." Then he added, "Let's see how we would answer the four questions based on this situation."

Julia thought carefully before she answered each question.

1. WHY is this report being written?

   "To find out how many customers are complaining about one product and exactly what they are complaining about."

2. For WHOM is this report being written?

   "Ms. Ohara, who may then turn the information over to the products department."

3. HOW will this report be used?

   "To correct something that is wrong with a product."

4. HOW MUCH should this report cover?

   "The number and nature of the customers' complaints about one product."

Activity A On a piece of paper, answer the four questions that determine purpose, based on this situation:

The sales director asks you to write a report that explains why the men's clothing division has been losing customers for the last three months.

Questions to Determine Purpose

1) WHY is this report being written?

2) For WHOM is this report being written?

3) HOW will this report be used?

4) HOW MUCH should this report cover?

Mr. Huyhen helps Julia organize information for her report.

Next, Julia and Mr. Huyhen worked on how to develop an action plan, which is a list of the steps necessary to complete a business report. It usually includes a statement of purpose. It lists major topics and suggests how to gather information on the topics. It also includes a schedule of dates for completing the steps.

Then Mr. Huyhen gave Julia this list of information that might be included in the action plan for any report.

General Information for an Action Plan

1. An explanation of what is being reported

2. A statement on why the report is needed

3. A list of what will be covered in the report and what limits have been placed on what will be covered

4. The definitions of words or terms that may not be familiar to people who will read the report

5. A schedule of where and how information will be gathered for the report

6. Possible conclusions and recommendations that will be proven based on the gathered information

---

Making an Outline

Mr. Huyhen told Julia, "At this point, you will want to make a brief outline to add to your action plan." He added, "You probably will change it some as you work, but an outline will help you organize your ideas." He explained that by this point, she also might have come up with some conclusions about the problem and ways the problem could be solved. If so, she should include those ideas on her outline as well. Mr. Huyhen concluded, "You'll also want to schedule your time so that the report is word processed, proofread, and copied—on or before the date that it is due."

Here is what Julia's action plan for the report on complaints about a product looked like.

An Action Plan
for a Business Report

1. **Purpose:** The purpose of this report is to find the number of and reasons for the complaints from customers regarding men's walking shorts (#345-687). This report is necessary in order to decide if the complaints are justified and, if they are, to make corrections in the manufacture of this item.

2. **Data gathering:** I will contact all members of the sales staff with a survey to determine the number and nature of the complaints.

3. **Rough outline:**
   I.   statement of purpose
   II. survey form
   III. results of survey
   IV. conclusions based on research
   V.   recommendations

4. **Schedule:**
   survey to be distributed: 6/12/01
   survey to be collected: 6/18/01
   collection of data complete: 6/20/01
   report written and revised by 6/25/01
   report submitted in final form: 7/1/01

Activity A Number your paper 1 to 8. If the statement is true, write *True* next to the number. If the statement is not true, write *False*.

1) The only thing you have to think about when you plan a business report is its purpose.

2) It is important to know who will read your report so that you can direct your information to that person or group of people.

3) An action plan will help you organize your report.

4) An action plan has three parts.

5) One part of an action plan is an explanation of what is being reported on.

6) You do not have to define terms because everyone reading the report should know what all of the words mean.

7) An action plan should contain a final outline.

8) It is important that an action plan contain a schedule that lists the dates when each step of the report will be completed.

Activity B On a piece of paper, write an action plan to help you to write a report on why the men's clothing division has been steadily losing customers for the last three months. Use the following information to help you.

· The report is due on Monday, March 26, 2001. You were given the job of writing the report on February 2.

· Look back at the previous pages in order to follow the action plan that Mr. Huyhen suggested to Julia.

Mr. Huyhen told Julia that getting the necessary information for a business report was probably the most important step in writing a report. "No matter how good a report looks and no matter how well the purpose is stated, if the information you gather is not complete or accurate, your report isn't worth the paper it's written on," he emphasized.

There are many ways you can gather information. One way is to take a **survey**. In a survey, you question people in order to collect information. You can also find information in books, magazines, newspapers, and even letters.

Survey

Finding information by asking people questions.

You can also conduct interviews or use observation as a source of information. For example, if a product is taking longer to make than it should, you might observe the workers who are making the product to see what is causing the delay.

The sources you use for your information often depend on the purpose of a report. Books and magazines, for example, will probably not help you find out why you are getting complaints about a product. However, they might help you to understand why your company is losing customers. For instance, books and magazines could tell you if your type of business is losing money all over the country. They could also help you to decide whether there is a market for a particular product or service. In addition, they could tell you what other companies are doing to solve the same kinds of problems that your company is experiencing.

Newspapers can give you information similar to that found in magazines and books, but since newspapers come out every day, information in them will be the latest information available. Local newspapers are especially good sources of information about local businesses and the economic conditions in your immediate area.

Activity A Number your paper 1 to 5. Each number stands for one of the five following topics. Next to each number, write the letters of the sources listed on page 241 that you could use to find information on that topic. (You will probably use more than one source for each topic, and you will use some sources more than once.)

Topic 1 Your report is about the latest trends in the use of robots in automobile plants. How effective are the robots? How much do they cost? What operations can they do? How many workers get laid off when robots are installed?

Topic 2 Your report is about whether certain changes should be made in a rowboat that your company makes. Will an improved rowboat improve sales? Will it have appeal to a larger group of customers? How will these changes affect the cost of the rowboat?

Topic 3 Your report is about how your company can improve the attendance of the workers. What have other companies done to improve attendance? What do workers in your company think would improve their attendance? What does your personnel department suggest.

Topic 4 Your report is about the use of a new fabric to cover the seats of the dining room chairs that your company makes. How sturdy is the new fabric? Will it increase the cost of the chairs? Is it stain resistant? Is it available in different colors and patterns?

Topic 5 Your report is about the possibility of building a restaurant in Daytona Beach, FL. How many restaurants are already located in Daytona Beach? What kind of restaurants are they? What is the economy like in Florida? What kinds of restaurants do people in Daytona Beach go to most often?

Sources of Information

a) fabric journals

b) restaurant journals

c) surveys of the sales staff and of your customers

d) books and magazines with articles about the use of robots

e) personal interviews with customers

f) letters to the Daytona Beach Chamber of Commerce asking for a list and description of all the restaurants

g) surveys to heads of companies who are using robots

h) magazines, pamphlets, and other publications on what companies do to improve attendance

i) calls to chair makers who have used this fabric

j) tests your company performs on this fabric

k) calls and letters to companies that have improved worker attendance

l) the production department of your company

m) magazine articles from magazines published in Florida

n) newspaper articles

o) magazines on making boats

p) surveys taken by personnel departments that asked workers what would improve their attendance

Julia gathered some data by surveying the sales manager.

"Now that you have gathered all of your information," Mr. Huyhen explained to Julia, "It is time to arrange your information in a logical order. In a business report, any order that makes sense can be used."

Mr. Huyhen explained that in a business report, information can be presented according to time, importance, space, cost, etc. He then explained that there are certain things that actually might determine the order used in a report.

When considering how to arrange your information, think about the people who will read your business report. They may be the kind of people who want to read all of the facts first and consider the conclusions last. Or, they may be just the opposite. They may want to see the conclusions first and then look at the information that led to those conclusions.

The topic of a report itself may be important in helping you decide the type of order you want to use. For example, if you are reporting on how good a certain fabric would be, you may want to arrange the information in the report so that the readers can easily compare the advantages of the new fabric to the fabric that is presently being used.

The way in which a report will be used may also help you decide on the order. In some business reports, charts and graphs are placed at the end of the report. In others, the charts and graphs appear on the same pages as the rest of the report because they are important to the understanding of the report. With this arrangement, the people reading the report are able to refer to the graphs and charts as they read the report.

Activity A   Number your paper 1 to 11. If the statement about business reports is true, write *True* next to the number. If the statement is not true, write *False*.

1) The order in which you arrange information in a report should depend only on who is going to read the report.

2) One acceptable way to arrange the information in a report is to give the conclusions first and the information that supports those conclusions later.

3) The topic of a report can be an important factor in deciding the order of information.

4) Graphs and charts can be placed at the back of the report.

5) Include graphs and charts as part of the report when they are well made and attractive.

6) Graphs and charts can be placed at the front of the report.

7) Sometimes you may want to arrange a report so that the readers can compare one product or one change with another.

8) Including charts and graphs as part of the report makes it possible for people to see some information as they read about it.

9) Selecting the right order for the information in a report is the easiest part of writing a report.

10) If charts are included just to summarize information, they could be placed at the back of the report.

11) Learning to choose the correct order for information in a report can make the difference between a successful or an unsuccessful report.

Outlining a Business Report

Mr. Huyhen told Julia that the best way to decide on the final order of information in a business report is to make an outline. Then he gave her this outline format so that she could refer to it when she made her own outline.

A Sample Outline

I. Introduction

    A. Purpose

    B. Survey of sales staff

        1. Number of complaints

        2. Nature of complaints

II. Explanation

    A. Interpretation of survey data

    B. Irregularities

III. Conclusions

IV. Recommendations

    A. Discontinue manufacture

    B. Redesign garment

The main parts of the outline were listed in the order that they would be presented in the report. Julia noticed that Roman numerals (I, II, III, etc.) were written on the lines beside the main parts of the report.

The details of each main part of the report were listed in the order that they would be presented. Each detail was indented on a separate line under the main part of the outline. Capital letters (A, B, C, etc.) were written on the lines beside the details.

Some of the details required additional information. If additional details were needed, each detail was indented on a separate line under the detail, in the order in which it would be talked about. Regular (Arabic) numbers (1, 2, 3, etc.) were written on the lines beside the additional details.

Julia noticed that the Roman numerals, capital letters, and regular numbers all had periods after them. The first letter of each main part, detail, and additional detail was capitalized.

Basically, an outline is a skeleton of your report. It serves as a means for organizing the topics you are going to include in a report. Using an outline will help you decide how to arrange main topics and details in the most effective way. For example, on a rough draft of an outline, you can rearrange ideas until you are able to include all of the related information in a logical order. Sometimes working with an outline will also show you that a few pieces of information you have gathered do not belong with the rest of the information.

Activity B   On your paper, write all of these parts of an outline in their correct order.

A. Grizzly	B. Polar
III. Fruit	2. Tiger Sharks
A. Sharks	A. Lemons
I. Bears	C. Rockfish
1. Great White Sharks	C. Oranges
II. Fish	B. Cherries
B. Tuna	D. Salmon

Activity C   On your paper, rewrite these parts of an outline in their correct order.

1. On-site studies	I. Introduction
B. Proposed renewal site	1. Survey of area for proposed new store
IV. Recommendations	
A. Purpose of report	B. Sources of information
2. Written survey of local merchants and customers	II. Explanation
	2. Projected sales
III. Conclusions	A. Survey data

Activity D On your paper, write the main topics for an outline from this list.

1) Statement of purpose

2) Sources of information

3) Recommendations

4) Survey forms

5) Store records

6) Conclusions

7) Interview with clerks

8) Explanation

Julia made a thorough outline of her report before she began writing it.

The next step for writing a business report that Julia worked on was explaining what the information means. Mr. Huyhen told her that sometimes when writing a report, she would have to explain what some of her facts meant or how they related to the problem. For example, after she explained what the problem was, she would then present the information that she had found. Finally, she would have to clearly explain what the new information had to do with the problem.

As Julia took notes, Mr. Huyhen explained that she would have to come to some conclusions about the information she had gathered and presented in her report. Conclusions are final, logical judgments that are based on the evidence or facts. For example, after having gathered facts about how good plastic washers are compared to rubber ones, you may have found that rubber washers are less likely to break. They provide a more drip-free closure and do not, like the plastic ones, create much wear and tear on the fixtures. Your conclusion then might be that rubber washers are the better ones to use. However, always remember that you must base any conclusions, or suggested ways of solving a problem, on the information you have gathered for your business report.

Making Recommendations

Then Mr. Huyhen told Julia that based on the information she had gathered and the conclusions she had reached, she would make some recommendations, or worthwhile suggestions, concerning what the company should do. For example, suppose that you found out that many companies offer cash bonuses for good attendance, and such bonuses help decrease absences. You could then reach the conclusion that the bonuses are not costing the companies any money because fewer workers call in sick. In fact, you could further conclude that four of the companies you surveyed said that they were saving money by giving these bonuses. You might then make the recommendation that your company adopt a policy of giving bonuses for outstanding attendance.

From the two examples described on page 247, you can see that getting the facts, interpreting those facts correctly, arriving at sound conclusions, and making good recommendations are all very important. If you make a recommendation without having all the facts, or if your recommendation is not based on the facts, your company could spend a great amount of money with no positive results.

Activity A   Number your paper 1 to 8. Then list the kinds of facts that you would have to have in order for each of these eight recommendations to be good ones.

1) Based on the information gathered, I recommend that the company use robots on the production line on an experimental basis.

2) As a result of this information, I recommend that the company not change the design of its rowboat.

3) The first recommendation is that workers be evaluated on their attendance as well as on other factors. Employees whose attendance is poor should not be eligible for pay increases.

4) The new fabric resists stains, has a long wearing life, and will increase the cost of each chair by only $5.00. I recommend that the new fabric be used to cover all dining room chairs.

5) I recommend that the company consider opening a restaurant in Daytona Beach only if a suitable site in the northwest section of the city can be found.

6) I recommend that the company continue to ship by train because that is the cheapest and most convenient method to use.

7) I recommend that the company get and advertise a toll-free telephone number for customers to use because this service is likely to increase business by 32%.

8) I recommend that the company stops producing men's shirts with button-down collars because only 6% of the men in this country wear them.

Writing a Business Report

Mr. Huyhen told Julia that after she had finished all the steps they had studied, she would be ready to write the rough draft of her business report. After she wrote it, she should then read through it carefully, making all needed changes and corrections so that the report is as good as it can possibly be. Then Mr. Huyhen told her that she should read through the final version of the word-processed report one more time, proofreading the final copy and eliminating any last errors.

Finally Mr. Huyhen said to Julia, "Usually you should make enough copies of your report for everyone involved with the report to get one, and it's important to keep a copy for yourself."

Activity B   Use the following ten steps as a guide to write a business report of your own.

1) Write a business report on a job or a career that interests you.

2) Write a clear statement of purpose. Be sure that your purpose answers the four questions below.
   - WHY is this report being written?
   - For WHOM is this report being written?
   - HOW will this report be used?
   - HOW MUCH should this report cover?

3) Prepare an action plan and collect information from several appropriate sources. For example, find out how good employment is in that field, what kind of salaries are paid, what chances there are for getting ahead in that field, and what kind of training or education you would need to get a job.

4) Arrange your information in a logical order.

5) Prepare an outline for your report.

6) Write your report.

7) Within the report, explain all terms and information clearly.

8) Include any conclusions you can draw as a result of the information in your report.

9) Include recommendations based on the information that you have gathered for your report.

10) Proofread the first draft of your report and correct any errors. Then make a final copy that is neat and accurate.

Oral business report

A report that is spoken out loud; a spoken account either based on outlined notes or read in full from a written report.

Mr. Huyhen told Julia, "If you ever have to present an **oral business report**, you would follow the same steps you used for preparing a written report. The only difference is that you may not have to write out the final report in full. In some cases, you might just present your oral report from outlined notes. At other times, though, you would still have to write out a written report that would be distributed. Then you would orally present only a summary of the report."

Then he added, "When giving an oral report, remember that your enthusiasm, use of language, voice, self-confidence, and appearance all play a part in how well your report is received."

Be Enthusiastic!

"I have seen many oral business reports fail," Mr. Huyhen told Julia, "not because of the information included in them but because of the way in which they were presented. For example, have you ever seen people give reports who look as though they aren't interested in what they are saying themselves?"

"Oh, yes," said Julia. "They are the kind of speakers who put me to sleep."

"I agree with you," Mr. Huyhen said. "They don't seem to care about what they are saying. Their lack of interest makes listeners wonder why they should care either. However, when speakers are excited, their listeners usually get excited, too!" Mr. Huyhen paused for a minute and then added, "Always speak with great enthusiasm, Julia. Look as if you are interested in what you are saying and the people to whom you are saying it. If you are enthusiastic, your listeners will believe that what you are saying is important!"

Use Language Well!

"When your oral business report is free of mistakes in grammar and pronunciation," Mr. Huyhen continued, "then your listeners will not be distracted and will pay attention to what you have to say. One way to eliminate some errors is to record your report and then listen for any mistakes that you tend to repeat. Then as you practice giving your report, work hard at eliminating those errors."

Speak Loudly and Clearly!

Mr. Huyhen explained that it is important to speak loudly and clearly when giving an oral report. "Your oral report will be meaningless if the people listening to you can't hear or understand what you are saying," he reminded Julia.

Be Self-Confident!

"If you are nervous, you might make your audience feel uncomfortable," Mr. Huyhen said. "Sometimes audiences interpret nervousness as a sign of not telling the truth." Then he advised her, "The best way to eliminate nervousness and be self-confident is to be well prepared. The more times you rehearse giving your report, the less nervous you will be when you present it to an audience."

Julia presented her findings at a sales meeting. She used the overhead projector to display some of the data.

Dress in a Businesslike Way!

"Finally, the way you look is also important," Mr. Huyhen pointed out to Julia. "You should wear business clothes and be neat and clean. However, it is not a good idea to overdress when giving a report. After all of your hard work to prepare an oral business report, you certainly don't want your audience to become distracted by inappropriate clothing or jewelry and not listen to what you have to say!"

Activity A   Number your paper 1 to 8. Then write the correct word or words that complete each sentence.

1) If your oral report shows that you think what you are saying is important, the _____ will think so, too.

2) Avoid making mistakes in _____ and in the way you _____ words so that the audience can pay attention to the information in your report.

3) A good way to eliminate mistakes is to _____ your report and then listen for mistakes that you tend to repeat.

4) It is important that you speak loudly enough so the _____ who are listening can _____ you.

5) You must also _____ words clearly so that they can be understood.

6) You should give the appearance of having _____ in yourself.

7) The best way to eliminate nervousness is to be well _____ .

8) You should wear _____ clothes and be _____ and clean.

You may reach a point in your career when you will need to gain some new skills if you want to advance in the company. In addition to taking some courses, you also could ask people you work with to teach you skills that they do well. Another possibility is to find books like this one in the library and teach yourself some new skills.

Some jobs more than others will require that you be able to write business reports. However, before you ever begin to write a report, you must consider the following:

- why the report is needed,
- for whom the report is needed,
- how the report will be used, and
- how much the report should cover.

Then you should develop an action plan for writing the report. This plan should include the purpose of the report, the steps for obtaining the needed information, a rough outline, and a schedule.

Once you have gathered your information, you should make a final outline that ends with conclusions and recommendations. Then you can begin writing your report. The final version of a written business report must be free of errors and easy to read.

If you are ever asked to give an oral report, you would prepare it in the same way that you would prepare a written report. However, if the oral report is supposed to be a summary of a written report you have done, then it should simply contain the main ideas of the written report.

For an oral report to be a success, you should be enthusiastic about your topic, use language correctly, speak loudly and clearly, make your audience feel that you are confident about what you are saying, and look businesslike.

Part A On your paper, fill in the missing parts of the Steps for Writing a Business Report on page 233. Then keep this paper in your notebook for future reference.

Steps for Writing a Business Report

1) Write answers to the following questions:

- Why _____ ?
- What _____ ?
- What _____ ?

2) Make an _____ for completing the report. Set _____ when each part of the plan should be completed. Develop a brief _____ .

3) Collect the _____ you need to answer your questions.

4) Make a final _____ that arranges your information in a logical order.

5) _____ or _____ any information your readers may not understand. At the end, draw _____ from your information and make _____ if needed.

6) Then follow these steps:

- Write a _____ of your report.
- _____ it carefully.
- Make any necessary _____ and _____ .
- Be sure that the final copy of your report is free of _____ .

Part B Number your paper 1 to 4. Then answer the questions on page 255 about the purpose of a report written about a toy called Quink, which is described below.

> Your company produces a fast-selling children's toy called a Quink. In fact, the company is having trouble keeping the stores that sell Quinks well supplied with stock. The head of the sales department has asked you to write a report that investigates ways that your company can increase its production of Quinks.

1) Why is this report being written?

2) For whom is this report being written?

3) How will this report be used?

4) How much should this report cover?

Part C On your paper, write an outline using the following information. Include main headings, subheadings, and minor details. (For help, review pages 244–245.)

the purpose: To decide whether to close the Piedmont Street store

It is losing business.

sources of information

sales records

researched information

conclusions

recommendations

remodel the store

introduction

It is losing customers.

It is losing money.

interviews with former customers

interviews with Piedmont Street employees

close the store

hire a new manager

Test Taking Tip If you have to read a paragraph before answering some questions, look over the paragraph quickly and then read the questions. Before answering the questions, go back to the paragraph and reread the parts that have the information you need to answer each question correctly.

Chapter

15

Handling Business Travel and Expenses

I f a new job involves any traveling, you might have to learn a few new related skills. After you start your new job, you also should begin to read professional journals so that you know as much about the business you're in as possible. Obviously, the more you know, the better employee you will be.

In Chapter 15, you will learn skills needed in responsible positions in a company—skills such as understanding transportation schedules and filling out expense account forms.

Goals for Learning

▶ To understand hotel rates and transportation schedules

▶ To know how to fill out an expense account form correctly

▶ To understand the importance of reading professional journals

In the previous chapter, Mr. Huyhen was training Julia Michaels for a new job. Because the new job was quite a step-up for Julia, it demanded some additional skills that she had not needed before. Still, Julia was excited because in the new job, she would be doing things she'd never had a chance to do before. She especially was looking forward to the opportunity to go on business trips.

Mr. Huyhen told Julia that he would show her what she needed to know in order to go on a business trip. He started by giving her a list of the hotels in the cities she would visit. Then he told her that he would help her interpret hotel rates and transportation schedules.

Hotel rate
The charge for renting a hotel room.

After each hotel name on the list was the **hotel rate** for a **single room**. He explained that the company's policy was to book a room in the hotel with the most reasonable rates unless no rooms were available in that hotel. Here is part of the list that Mr. Huyhen gave to Julia.

Single room
A hotel room for one person.

Hotel Rates

In New York City:

The Newton	$125.00
The Howard	$158.00
The Sherwood	$132.00

What hotel should Julia contact first if she were planning to travel to New York City for her company? What is the last hotel she should try?

Double room
A hotel room for two people.

A room designed for two people is called a **double room**. Most hotels charge more if two or more people stay in a room.

Activity A Number your paper 1 to 7. Then write short answers to the following questions about this list of rates for the Hotel Crown.

The Hotel Crown
1128 Strand Avenue
Chicago, IL 60611

Rates

*Single room, double bed	$97.00 per day
*Single room, queen-sized bed	$112.00 per day
*Double room, queen-sized bed	$120.00 per day
*Double room, two queen-sized beds	$145.00 per day

For extra person in room, add $10.00.

1) What hotel offers these rates?

2) Where is the hotel located?

3) How many possible types of reservations could you make?

4) What is the least that a single person can pay to stay at the hotel for one night?

5) If a husband and wife shared a single room with a queen-sized bed, what would they pay for one night?

6) If two business associates were sharing a room with two beds, what would they pay for one night?

7) If a husband, wife, and their son stayed for one night in a room with two queen-sized beds, what would they pay?

Transportation schedule

A chart or table that shows the arrival and departure times of trains, buses, planes, etc.

Transportation Schedule Abbreviations

Because Julia would be doing quite a bit of traveling if she got the new job, she would also have to know how to read **transportation schedules**. Because these schedules could be confusing due to the many abbreviations they contain, Mr. Huyhen gave Julia this list of transportation abbreviations.

Transportation Abbreviations

ar. *or* arr.	——	arrives at
dp. *or* dep.	——	departs at
E.T.A.	——	estimated time of arrival
a	——	a.m.
p	——	p.m.
m	——	midnight
n	——	noon
ET	——	Eastern Time
CT	——	Central Time
MT	——	Mountain Time
PT	——	Pacific Time
M	——	Monday
T	——	Tuesday
W	——	Wednesday
TH	——	Thursday
F	——	Friday
SA	——	Saturday
SU	——	Sunday

Notice that in some cases, two abbreviations are given. However, a transportation company would use only one of these abbreviations on its schedules. For example, Travcon Airlines might use *arr.* to stand for *arrival*, while Mountain Airlines might use *ar.*

Mr. Huyhen also showed Julia the transportation schedule shown on page 261.

Chicago to
New York City

Nonstop Flight #	Dep.			E.T.A.			Notes
176	5:32	a	CT	7:49	a	ET	M–F
184	6:18	a	CT	8:35	a	ET	SA only
246	7:23	a	CT	9:40	a	ET	M–F
273	9:45	a	CT	12:02	n	ET	SA,SU
350	1:17	p	CT	3:34	p	ET	M–F
381	7:43	p	CT	10:00	p	ET	SU only
397	10:00	p	CT	12:07	m	ET	M–F

Activity B   Number your paper 1 to 10. Then write short answers to these questions based on the above transportation schedule.

1) What city do these planes leave from?

2) What city do these planes travel to?

3) If you needed to be in New York City in time for a 9:00 A.M. meeting on Monday, which flight would you take?

4) If you wanted to get to New York by 7:00 A.M. on Wednesday, April 4, what flight would you take? On what day?

5) Suppose you have a meeting in Chicago on Sunday that will be over at noon. It takes you one hour to get to the airport. What is the earliest flight you could take to get to New York?

6) What time does the 10:00 P.M. flight from Chicago get to New York?

7) Can you take Flight 273 on Thursday?

8) If the Notes column had *T, W, Th* listed next to a flight, on what days could you take that flight?

9) Since the time in New York City is an hour later than it is in Chicago, how long is Flight 397?

10) What is the estimated time of arrival of Flight 350?

Expense account form

A form on which employees list business expenses so that the company can pay them back.

Receipts

The written statements or forms that report the receipt of goods and noting any payment.

Julia saved all of the receipts from her business trip.

Mr. Huyhen explained to Julia that the Linsey-Wolsey Company does not give expense money ahead of time. However, once Julia returned from a trip, she could fill out an **expense account form** in order to be repaid the money she had spent for business purposes on the trip. He emphasized that she would have to include **receipts** from the trip along with the form.

He stressed, for example, that she would have to get receipts for her transportation costs. If Julia used her own car, she would need receipts for gasoline, tolls, parking, and any other related expenses. If she used other means of transportation, she would have to supply receipts for planes, trains, buses, subways, and/or taxicabs.

"Do I need receipts for my meals?" Julia asked.

Mr. Huyhen assured her that she should keep receipts not only for her meals but also for such expenses as her hotel room and any business telephone calls. He added, "The company does not reimburse expenses for personal phone calls, entertainment, rent, or clothing."

Activity A   Number your paper 1 to 15. Then write *Yes* after each item that you could include on an expense account form—if you kept your receipts. Write *No* if you could not include the item.

1) breakfast

2) train fare

3) a new belt

4) a suitcase

5) taxi fare

6) 35¢ toll

7) a toothbrush

8) parking

9) dinner

10) a long-distance call to a friend

11) gasoline used in driving for business

12) dinner for a customer

13) dinner for a friend

14) plane ticket

15) hotel room

Activity B   Number your paper 1 to 3. Then write short answers to these questions.

1) Why do you think some companies do not give employees money before they take a business trip?

2) Why would a company repay only those items for which an employee has a receipt?

3) Why would a company pay for taking a customer to dinner but not pay for taking a friend?

Destination
The place where one is going or has gone.

Lodging
The place where one stays; a hotel or motel room.

Mileage
The number of miles traveled on a given trip.

Reimbursement
A repayment of money paid by a worker for business expenses.

Filling Out an Expense Account Form

Mr. Huyhen took out an expense account form that the Linsey-Wolsey Company uses. He explained to Julia which information went into each section. She wrote notes in each section so that she would remember how to complete a blank form. She included the definitions for the words **destination**, **mileage**, **lodging**, and **reimbursement**. Here is the form Mr. Huyhen gave to Julia.

Linsey-Wolsey Company
Expense Account Form

Name of Employee _____ *my name* _____

Social Security # _____ *my Social Security number* _____

Dates Expenses Occurred _ *from* _ *to* _____

Destination _____ *where I went* _____

Purpose _____ *why I went* _____

Use of Privately Owned Car If I use my own car, I get 32¢ per mile.		Taxi, Bus, Plane, Train, Subway	Meals	Phone Calls
Mileage # of miles traveled	$@32¢/mile 32¢ × number of miles	total of fares	total cost of meals	total cost of business calls
Lodging	Miscellaneous		TOTAL Reimbursement Request	
total of hotel or motel cost	anything else I spent on business		total of mileage or fares, meals, business calls, hotels and miscellaneous	

NO REIMBURSEMENT WILL BE MADE WITHOUT RECEIPTS

Mr. Huyhen reminded Julia that she had to be sure to fill in the name, Social Security number, dates expenses occurred, destination, and purpose sections of the expense form. He explained that the Linsey-Wolsey Company would need that information for her expense record. This record would be needed when the company figured out the taxes it had to pay. Julia's Social Security number would help the company keep track of the amount it paid Julia for salary and the amount it reimbursed her for expenses.

Activity C Number your paper 1 to 14. Then match the terms from an expense account form in the first column with their descriptions in the second column.

Term	Description
1) Name of Employee	**a)** total cost of meals
2) Social Security #	**b)** where you went
3) Dates Expenses Occurred	**c)** your name
4) Destination	**d)** a total of the expenses for mileage or fares, meals, business telephone calls, lodgings, and miscellaneous
5) Purpose	
6) Use of Privately Owned Car	**e)** any use you made of your own car related to the business trip
7) Mileage	
8) $ at 32¢ per mile	**f)** dates you were on the business trip
9) Taxi, Bus, Plane, Train, Subway	**g)** number of miles traveled in your own car
10) Meals	**h)** anything else spent on business that does not belong in any of the other categories
11) Phone Calls	
12) Lodging	
13) Misc.	
14) Total Reimbursement Request	**i)** total cost of business calls
	j) total hotel or motel cost
	k) reason for taking the trip
	l) 32¢ times the number of miles
	m) your Social Security number
	n) fare for taxi, train, bus, subway, or plane

Activity D Number your paper 1 to 10. Then write short answers to these questions about business travel and expenses.

1) Suppose you used your own car for a business trip, and your company reimburses you at the rate of 35¢ per mile. How much would you get back if you drove 118 miles?

2) Why do you think some employers want to know the dates you were away on a business trip?

3) Look on page 264 at the expense account form that the Linsey-Wolsey Company uses. What are you supposed to write in the column that says, "Taxi, Bus, Train, Subway, Plane?"

4) How can you figure out the total amount of money you spent for meals during a trip?

5) How would keeping a log or business diary help you to figure out the business telephone calls you made?

6) What does *lodging* mean? What would you put in that column?

7) List at least three miscellaneous expenses you might include on an expense account form.

8) The expense account form that the Linsey-Wolsey Company uses asks for *destination*. What does that term mean?

9) If you were asked for the purpose of your trip, do you think it would be enough to write, "business"? Explain your answer.

10) Why do you think you need to include your Social Security number on an expense account form?

Professional journal

Magazines related to business in general or to specific areas of business.

Mr. Huyhen explained to Julia that employees who really want to get ahead should read as much as they can about business in general—as well as the specific business they are in. He said, "The more you know about what is going on in the business world, the more valuable you are to your company."

Then Mr. Huyhen gave Julia a **professional journal** about managing businesses. Here is part of an article in that magazine.

Too much socializing by the employees can cause problems for some businesses. Here are some ways in which this problem can be avoided.

1. The leaders of the company should set a good example. If they want to discourage socialization by their employees, then they should not be seen socializing.

2. The leaders of the company should be observant. Generally, business conversations and telephone calls do not take much time. When you see employees talking together or speaking on the phone for long periods of time, you can be pretty sure that they are socializing.

3. Those people who are over socializing should be confronted directly. Some behavior changes should be negotiated.

4. The leaders should administer this kind of policy fairly.

After Julia had read this part of the journal article, she and Mr. Huyhen talked about the ideas in it. Mr. Huyhen said that even though this article had nothing to do with the kind of business that the Linsey-Wolsey Company does, it certainly addressed a problem the company has. Julia said, "It gives me some ideas about handling employees that I will supervise on my new job."

Julia began to see how knowing something about this problem of socializing might help her in her job. Now she would be able to offer suggestions if her new supervisor asked her about the problem. She could even quote from an article that she had read.

Activity A   Number your paper 1 to 7. Then after you reread the article that Mr. Huyhen gave Julia, write short answers to these questions about the article.

1) What problem does this article discuss?

2) According to this article, who is doing the socializing—the bosses or the workers?

3) What does *socializing* mean?

4) Why is it important for the leaders of a company to set a good example?

5) If you observe different employees talking or making calls, what might you find out?

6) How does this article suggest that a supervisor handle this problem?

7) Why is it important for a supervisor to be fair about solving this problem?

Activity B   Suppose you were a supervisor. Why would you want your employees to read as many professional journals and magazines as possible? Write a short paragraph that gives several reasons why reading professional journals is important.

Chapter Summary

As you receive promotions, your job responsibilities often change. You may find, for example, that your new job requires a certain amount of traveling. As a rule, most companies pay all of your expenses for business travel. However, you must keep track of how much you spend by keeping your receipts for such expenses as plane fare, hotel rooms, and meals.

If you travel as part of your job, you will have to follow schedules for planes, trains, subways, and buses. You will also have to know how to fill out expense account forms if you want to be reimbursed for your business expenses.

Finally, knowing what is going on in the business world will help you get ahead in your job. You need to know what new things are happening and what is working well in other businesses. One way to keep informed is to read professional journals. Being informed about your business will let you make helpful suggestions and will show your supervisor that you are interested in your job and in your company.

Part A Number your paper 1 to 10. Then write short answers for the following questions about this transportation schedule.

Louisville to

Los Angeles	Nonstop					
Flight #	Dp.			Ar.		Notes
32	8:15	a	ET	9:35	a	PT	M-F only
57	11:33	a	ET	12:53	n	PT	SA,SU only
144	3:15	p	ET	4:35	p	PT	M-F only
76	4:10	p	ET	5:30	p	PT	Th, F, SA only
117	7:22	p	ET	8:32	p	PT	T,W only

1) What city do these planes leave from?

2) What city do they travel to?

3) Do they make any stops? How do you know?

4) On what days can you take Flight 57?

5) If you needed to be in Los Angeles for a business meeting at 1:00 P.M. on Tuesday, what flight would you take out of Louisville?

6) Which flights run every weekday?

7) Which flight runs only on weekends?

8) Mary is flying to Los Angeles for her sister's wedding on Sunday. She can afford to stay only one night. Which flight or flights could she take?

9) Bill has an important business meeting in Los Angeles at 9:00 A.M. on Tuesday morning. Which flight should he take? When does it leave? What time is it in Louisville when he arrives in Los Angeles?

10) You can get a cheaper ticket if you take Flight 76. What days can you take that flight? What time would you leave Louisville? What time would you arrive in Los Angeles?

Part B Number your paper 1 to 15. If the statement is true, write *True* next to the number. If it is not true, write *False*.

1) If you use your own car for business travel, you need to keep track of the miles you travel.

2) Many companies will repay you if you have to take a taxi.

3) You will be repaid for all of the telephone calls you make.

4) On an expense account form, you can include a new suitcase under miscellaneous expenses.

5) You can include paper you bought to make a chart for the report that you are doing for your company.

6) The term *reimburse* means *to repay someone for expenses.*

7) Some expense account forms ask for the dates and destination of your travel.

8) The purpose of your travel is the specific reason why you went on the trip.

9) Making a report and getting an order from a customer are two good reasons for making a business trip.

10) Companies seldom require receipts for expenses because they trust their employees.

11) The term *mileage* means *the number of miles* that you drove on business.

12) If you drive your own car, you will be reimbursed for gasoline, tolls, parking, and an oil change.

13) Only managers should read professional journals.

14) A company will reimburse you for any plane or train fares.

15) Most companies give a flat rate for the number of miles you drive in your own car.

Test Taking Tip

If you have to choose the correct ending to a sentence, combine the first part of the sentence with each ending. Then choose the one that best completes the statement.

Glossary

A

Abbreviations—the shortened forms of written words; for example, *req.* for *required* (p. 2)

Accident report—a form that must be completed when an employee is injured on the job (p. 225)

Action plan—a list of the steps necessary to complete a business report; it usually includes a statement of purpose, methods for gathering information, rough outline of procedures, and schedule of dates for completing each step (p. 233)

Address—the place where a person lives or works (p. 67)

Adult education—classes or correspondence courses for adults; students may take courses to learn special skills such as keyboarding or woodworking, to earn a high school diploma, and/or to focus on a certain subject such as a foreign language (p. 207)

Agenda—a list of topics to be discussed (in a given order) at a meeting (p. 189)

Allowances—things the government will consider when deciding what amount of money will be withheld from a person's salary as income tax (See **Personal allowances** for examples.) (p. 110)

Alphabetical order—arranged in the order of the letters of the alphabet (*A, B, C,* etc.) (p. 5)

Amount—on a sales slip, the product of the number purchased times the unit price; for example, *5 items × $2.40 for each = an amount of $12.00* (p. 159)

Apprenticeship program—a work program in which people learn a trade by working on the job; they gain practical experience under the supervision of skilled workers (p. 13)

Area code—a three-digit number that identifies each telephone service area in the United States (p. 184)

B

Bar graph—a diagram that uses lines and shaded areas to present and compare information (p. 150)

Benefits—payments or services provided for workers by a company; for example, vacation, retirement, and health insurance (p. 10)

Body—the part of a letter that tells why it is being written (p. 21)

Business machines—equipment used by many companies; for example, a fax machine, a personal computer, or a ten-key calculator (p. 45)

Business report—a written record that presents investigated facts about a business situation and that offers conclusions and recommendations based on those facts (p. 232)

C

Career objectives—what people eventually hope to become or achieve in their profession; for example, to become a master plumber or a computer programmer (p. 48)

Catalog—a listing of items arranged in a systematic way; a description of these items is often included (p. 166)

Chart—a diagram that presents information in a table or list (p. 149)

Checklist—a list people can go over to see if they have completed all the steps they had wanted to accomplish (p. 58)

Classified ads—advertisements that are listed in the newspaper in different groups; for example, ads for cars would be listed together in one section, ads for pets in another, and job openings in another (p. 2)

College—a form of schooling beyond high school where people take courses and earn degrees; on a job application, a term referring to the name of the college or university the applicant attended (p. 67)

College application—a form used to request admission to a college as a degree candidate (p. 204)

Communication—the way or ways people let others know how they feel about something; there can be verbal communication (such as speaking and writing) and nonverbal communication (such as body language) (p. 103)

Company—on a job application, the term referring to the place where the applicant works or the places where the applicant has worked before (p. 68)

Complimentary close—the part of a letter that provides a polite ending; for example, *Sincerely,* or *Respectfully yours,* (p. 22)

Computer printout—a printed record produced automatically by a computer (p. 163)

Conclusions—final, logical judgments based on facts (p. 232)

Counselor—a person at an employment agency or job placement office who helps another person to find a job; a person who gives advice to someone (p. 13)

Course—the subject in which a person majored in school; for example, high school programs might include academic, college preparatory, business, auto mechanics, general course, etc. (p. 68)

Course description—an explanation of what is taught in a course; usually found in a catalog (p. 202)

Course number—a number given to a course to show that it is different from other courses (p. 202)

Course title—the name of a course: for example, *Computers for the Beginner* or *Computers I* (p. 202)

Credit—points given by a college to a student who has successfully finished a course (p. 202)

D

Date—the month, day, and year used in letters to tell when they were written (p. 21)

Deductible—a clause in an insurance policy that makes the policy holder responsible for paying a certain amount of a loss; for example, if a person's car is damaged in an accident, that person might have to pay the first $100 to have it fixed and the insurance company would pay the rest (p. 192)

Deduction—an expense considered when determining taxable income; a person does not have to pay income taxes on expenses such as donations to a charity, qualifying home mortgage interest payments, state and local taxes, etc. (p. 111)

Degree—an award granted after completing a two-year community or four-year regular college; for example, an *Associate of Arts degree (A.A.), Bachelor of Arts degree (B.A.), Bachelor of Science degree (B.S.),* etc. (p. 68)

Degree candidate—a person seeking to complete a degree program and earn a college diploma (p. 204)

Degree desired—the degree program that a student is working to complete; for example, an *Associate of Arts (A.A.), Bachelor of Arts (B.A.), Bachelor of Science (B.S.),* etc. (p. 202)

Dependents—children or other people who may not work and who count on a wage earner for over half of their needs (food, clothing, shelter, etc.) (p. 111)

Destination—the place where a person is going or has been (p. 264)

Disconnected—not connected; a term describing a telephone connection that has been severed or ended (p. 187)

Double room—a hotel or motel room for two people (p. 258)

E

Employment agency—a company that is in the business of helping people find jobs; most agencies charge a fee to either the employer or the employee for these services (p. 12)

Evaluation—a judgment about how well a worker does a job; many companies use a standard form on which to record, on a regular basis, a judgment of the employee; this evaluation can be used to recommend workers for promotions, raises, or firing (p. 121)

Exemption—some reason why certain sums of money do not have to be taken from a person's salary for income tax; it might be because that person has a child or parent to support (p. 111)

Expense account form—a form on which employees list business expenses so that the company can pay them back (p. 262)

Experience—a term referring to jobs that people have held; on a résumé, job experiences usually include the dates a person was employed, company names and addresses, job titles, duties, supervisors, and reasons for leaving (p. 48)

Extension—an extra telephone connected to the principal line; the number to connect to such a telephone line (p. 184)

Extracurricular—a term used to describe activities beyond the regular school curriculum; for example, sports teams, school newspaper, school play or musical, debating club, etc. (p. 49)

F

Fact sheet—information about a person who is looking for a job; it should include personal, career, and educational information—plus references; a fact sheet will help in writing résumés and in completing job applications (p. 65)

Fax machine—a business machine that sends copies of written documents through the telephone lines (p. 168)

Follow-up letter—a second letter written to correct a mistake, to give or ask for additional information, or to suggest solutions to a problem (p. 171)

Full block style—a form of business writing in which all parts of a letter are written against the left margin; no paragraphs are indented (p. 23)

G

Good impression—thinking well of people because they use proper behavior, language, etc. (p. 84)

Group insurance—insurance purchased for a large group of people, such as the employees of a company; the cost of group insurance is less expensive than individual insurance (p. 218)

H

Help-wanted ads—advertisements for employment or job openings (p. 2)

Hotel rate—the charge for renting a hotel room (p. 258)

Human resources—the part of a company that deals with employees; human resources hires people and keeps records about how well they do their jobs; another name for this department is *personnel* (p. 218)

I

Immediate supervisor—the person who has direct charge of an employee; a boss (p. 121)

Indented—set in from the margin of the page; paragraphs are indented in the modified block style of business letters (p. 27)

Index—a list of items that are found in a book with the page numbers where those items can be found; an index is usually found in the back of a book (p. 147)

Inside address—the part of a letter that includes the complete name and address of the person or company where the letter is being sent (p. 21)

Insurance coverage—benefits included within the scope of an insurance policy or protective plan; the risks covered by the terms of an insurance contract (p. 132)

Insuree (employee)—on an insurance form, the name of the worker or person who has the insurance (p. 220)

Intercom—a two-way system that has a microphone and a loudspeaker that allows people in nearby office areas to talk to each other without leaving their desks (p. 182)

Internal Revenue Service (IRS)—the government agency in charge of collecting taxes (p. 110)

Interviewer—the person in charge of an interview (p. 86)

Inventory—the amount of goods or materials on hand; stock (p. 158)

Invoice—a form containing a list of the goods sold; some invoices also have the price of each item and the conditions of sale (p. 160)

Item number—the figure used to identify each separate item sold by a company; used in inventory lists, in catalogs, on sales slips, etc. (p. 159)

Job application—a form used in making a request to be hired (p. 64)

Job interview—a meeting during which the person doing the hiring asks questions and rates the answers of the person applying for a job (p. 13)

Job placement office—a city or state office where people can get help in finding a job; public job placement offices do not usually charge for their services (p. 12)

Key words—important words that give the main idea; clues or aids used to help people remember information (p. 137)

Labels—words or abbreviations attached to objects in order to identify or describe them (p. 151)

Letter of application—a letter used in making a request to be hired; people sometimes send a copy of their résumé along with a letter of application (p. 20)

Locker—a cupboard or compartment that may be closed with a lock; a compartment where a person can store personal belongings (p. 119)

Lodging—on an expense account form, the term used to refer to the place where a person stays—such as a hotel or motel (p. 264)

Logical order—the arrangement of information in an order that makes sense; for example, according to time, importance, space, cost, etc. (p. 233)

Major headings—the most important items in a list; in an index, these items are usually typed against the left margin and begin with capital letters (p. 147)

Margin—the outside edge of a page on which there is no writing or printing (p. 24)

Medical insurance—protection to help pay bills caused by illness or injury; if the person who carries the insurance pays premiums regularly, then the insurance company agrees to pay certain medical bills (p. 218)

Message—a written or a spoken form of communication (p. 179)

Mileage—on an expense account form, the term used to refer to the number of miles traveled on a given trip (p. 264)

Minutes—the official written record of what happens at a meeting (p. 188)

Modified block style—in this form of business letter, the return address, date, complimentary close, and signature are lined up near the center of the page; paragraphs are indented (p. 26)

Motion—a formal call for action or a proposal made at a meeting; for example, someone might say, "I make a motion that we spend $10,000 for advertising." (p. 188)

N/A—not applicable; a term used on job applications when a section does not apply to the person applying for the job (p. 75)

Objective—not influenced by personal feelings, prejudices, etc.; for example, a person might make an objective decision based on facts and nothing else (p. 189)

Operator—a person who connects and transfers telephone calls (p. 85)

Oral business report—a report that is spoken out loud; a spoken account either based on outlined notes or read in full from a written report (p. 250)

Oral directions—instructions given by word of mouth; spoken rather than written orders (p. 137)

Order—the placing of topics or events in a reasonable arrangement; the order could be by time, importance, space, cost, etc. (p. 46)

Order letters—letters written to order merchandise from a company (p. 168)

Outline—a summary of a written work; a preliminary account of a project that serves as a means for organizing the topics to be included (p. 233)

Patient—the name of the person who is being treated medically (p. 220)

Pay week—one pay period of seven days; it may run from Monday to Sunday, Tuesday to Monday, etc. (p. 128)

Personal allowances—things the government will consider when deciding what amount of money will be withheld from people's salary as income tax; people can claim from none to several allowances on their W-4 form—depending on whether they are single or married, whether their spouse works, whether they have dependents or more than one job, etc. (p. 110)

Personal information—the part of a résumé that includes a person's name, address, telephone number, etc. (p. 48)

Personal qualifications—traits that help a person meet job requirements; for example, having a good attendance record, and following directions well (p. 88)

Personnel—the part of a company that deals with the employees; personnel hires people and keeps records about how well they do their jobs; another name for this department is *human resources* (p. 82)

Place of birth—the city, state, and country where a person was born (p. 71)

Position—on a job application, a term referring to a job or job title; the name of the job that an employee does or the work for which a person has been hired; for example, *short-order cook* or *receptionist* (p. 129)

Post office abbreviations—two-letter forms of state names used by the United States Post Office; for example, *TN* for *Tennessee* (p. 37)

Premium—the amount of money paid for insurance protection (p. 218)

Preprinted answer sheet—a form on which students mark answers to tests by filling in circles, circling letters, etc. (p. 210)

Probation—a period of time new workers have to prove that they can do the job; many workers are on probation for the first six months that they are on the job (p. 114)

Professional journal—a magazine related to business in general (management policies, interview guidelines, etc.) and to specific trade areas (medicine, retail sales, real estate, etc.) (p. 267)

Promotion—a raise in rank or position; the change may include an increase in pay (p. 121)

R

Receipts—the written statements or forms acknowledging the receipt of goods and noting any payment (p. 262)

Receptionist—a person whose job it is to answer phone calls, greet the public, answer questions, direct people to offices, etc.; the receptionist is often the first contact people have with a company (p. 102)

Recommendations—suggestions based on information gathered and conclusions reached (p. 232)

Reference books—books containing useful facts or information, such as a dictionary, encyclopedia, or atlas (p. 7)

References—people who know another person and who can describe the kind of person he or she is, the things that person does well, and/or the way that person gets along with others; references can be friends, teachers, clergy, or past employers (p. 31)

Registration form—a form used to sign up for college courses (p. 203)

Reimbursement—repayment of money to a worker for business expenses (p. 264)

Resolution—a formal statement of a decision or an expression of opinion voted by an official body or assembled group (p. 188)

Résumé—a summary of a person's career and qualifications that is used when that person is applying for a job (p. 44)

Return address—the part of a letter that includes the street address, city, state, and ZIP code of the writer; also the part of an envelope that includes the name, street address, city, state, and ZIP code of the writer; the return address is written in the upper left-hand corner of the envelope (p. 20)

Rough draft—the first copy of a piece of writing; that piece will be revised, proofread, and corrected before a final copy is made (p. 51)

S

Safety equipment—protective gear required on a job; for example, safety goggles, heavy work gloves, and hard hats (p. 225)

Salary—a fixed amount of money paid on a regular basis for work done (p. 10)

Sales slip—a form used by most retail stores as a record of a purchase or sale (p. 158)

Sales tax—a tax figured on the cost of a sale; it is a percentage of the purchase price of the goods bought and is collected by the company that sells the goods (p. 159)

Salutation—the part of a letter that greets the person to whom the letter is addressed; for example, *Dear Ms. Evans:* or *Dear Sir:* (p. 21)

Schedule—a plan that shows the time and the order of each job; it can also show who does the job (p. 134)

School records—files containing information about a person's grades, standard test scores, attendance, etc. (p. 65)

Second—a statement that a person agrees to or supports a motion under discussion at a meeting (p. 188)

Section—one particular class, out of several, that may be offered of the same course (p. 202)

Sexual harassment—doing or saying something sexual to someone who does not welcome it (p. 116)

Shift—a scheduled period of work or duty; for example, 3:00 P.M. to 11:00 P.M., 11:00 P.M. to 7:00 A.M., 7:00 A.M. to 3:00 P.M., etc. (p. 130)

Signature—a handwritten (rather than typed or printed) name on a letter; also the part of the letter that identifies the writer; business letters often include a handwritten signature above the typed full name (p. 22)

Single room—a hotel or motel room for one person (p. 258)

Slang—the use of coarse, nonstandard, incorrect, or informal language; for example, *yeah* or *ain't* (p. 88)

Social Security number—a nine-digit number used to identify Americans for such government purposes as taxes, unemployment payments, old-age benefits, and survivor benefits (p. 65)

Spouse—a person's husband or wife (p. 111)

Subtotal—the sum of part of a series of figures; on a sales slip, the subtotal is the sum of the amounts of various items purchased (figured before sales tax is added) (p. 159)

Supervisor—a person who is in charge of others; a boss (p. 64)

Survey—to question people in order to collect information (p. 239)

T

Telephone directory—a book or collection of names, addresses, and telephone numbers (p. 7)

Time card—a card used with a time clock to record an employee's starting and quitting times during each day on the job (p. 114)

Toll-free—without cost; often referring to a telephone number that begins with the digits 800 (p. 220)

Tone—the inflection or pitch of words used to express meaning, mood, or feeling (p. 91)

Total—on a sales slip, the sales tax is added to the subtotal to give the total amount of the purchase (p. 159)

Trade manuals—handbooks explaining a particular skilled job, such as plumbing or electrical work; books describing new tools, methods, or products in a particular trade area (p. 144)

Transfer—to switch a business telephone call to another department or person (p. 187)

Transportation schedule—a chart or table that shows the arrival and the departure times of trains, buses, and planes (p. 260)

U

Undergraduate degree—a degree offered for completing a course of study in a college program, such as a two-year *Associates of Arts (A.A.)* degree or a four-year *Bachelor of Arts (B.A.)* or *Bachelor of Science (B.S.)* degree (p. 201)

Unit price—the cost for one item, box, dozen, gallon, pound, etc. (p. 159)

V

Voice mail—an electronic system that records telephone messages that are played back later by the recipient (p. 182)

Volunteer—a person who provides a service freely and without being paid (p. 56)

W

W-4 form—a form put out by the Internal Revenue Service to decide the amount of money that will be taken out of a person's pay for income tax; workers must complete this form when they are hired (p. 110)

Withholding—an amount of money a company subtracts from an employee's salary; this part of the salary is paid directly to the IRS as part or all of that person's income tax (p. 110)

Witnesses—the names of people who saw an accident and could tell what happened (p. 225)

Workers' compensation—insurance that reimburses an employer for benefits that must be paid to an employee who is disabled or injured during the course of employment (p. 223)

Work schedule—a plan that shows the exact hours or shifts each employee will work during a given pay period (p. 130)

Workstation—the place where an employee works or does a certain part of the job (p. 116)

Y

Yellow Pages—the section of a telephone book that lists businesses in alphabetical order by kind of business; for example, places to eat are all listed under the heading, *Restaurants* (p. 7)

Z

ZIP code—a number used to identify postal delivery areas in the United States (p. 20)

Index